Absolutely Write!
Teaching the
Craft Elements of Writing

Absolutely Write!
Teaching the
Craft Elements of Writing

Tommy Thomason and Carol York

with Foreword by
Bill Martin Jr.

Christopher-Gordon Publishers, Inc.
Norwood, Massachusetts

Copyright Acknowledgments

Forest in the Clouds by Sneed Collard used by permission of Charlesbridge Publishing, Inc.

Teacher vignettes used with permission of the teacher.

Poems Perfect Attendance from Rainbows, Head Lice and Pea-Green Tile, and Mirror Image by Brod Bagart, New Orleans, Louisiana. Copyright © by Brod Bagart. Used by permission of Brod Bagart.

Quotes from Buffalo Dreams by Kim Doner, Tulsa, Oklahoma. Copyright © by Kim Doner. Used with permission of Kim Doner.

"The Youngest of Writers" from Florida Primary Educator by Marcia S. Freeman. Copyright © by Marcia Freeman. Used by permission of Marcia S. Freeman.

Essay by Vicki Spandel used by permission of Vicki Spandel, writing consultant to Great Source Education Group.

Line from Best Friends by Steven Kellogg used with permission of Steven Kellogg.

Excerpts from All Over but the Shoutin' by Rick Bragg, 1997, New York, NY: Pantheon Books. Copyright © 1997 by Rick Bragg. Used by permission of Pantheon Books, a division of Random House, Inc.

Excerpt from Old Devil Wind used with permission of Bill Martin, Jr.

Excerpt from Storm on the Desert by Carolyn Lesser, copyright 1997 reprinted with permission of Harcourt, Inc.

Excerpt from SHREK! by William Steig. Copyright 1990 by William Steig. Reprinted with permission of Farrar, Straus and Giroux, LLC.

The Bill Harp Professional Teacher's Library
An Imprint of
Christopher-Gordon Publishers, Inc.
1502 Providence Highway, Suite 12
Norwood, MA 02062
800-934-8322

Printed in the United States of America

10 9 8 7 6 5 4 3 2 1   05 04 03 02 01

Library of Congress Catalog Card Number: 2001095881
ISBN: 1-929024-40-1

Dedication

To our friend and mentor Bill Martin Jr., whose love of
language and pioneering work with young writers
has left an example for a whole generation
of writing teachers.

Table of Contents

Foreword

Bill Martin Jr.

I just read a marvelous new book by Tommy Thomason and Carol York that re-confirms what I believe about the process of leading students into writing in a joyous, fulfilling way.

Absolutely Write! helped me realize what I already knew about writing but perhaps did not know I knew. This is important because in it lies an important point for writing teachers—you have to trust your instincts as a writer as you lead students into the world of writing.

As a writer, I was heavily influenced by Walt Whitman, Mark Twain, and Robert Frost. Thomason and York have crafted a wonderful chapter, "Learning to Write from the Authors You Love," that will help teachers of writing and developing authors benefit from the styles of their favorite published authors.

As a writer, I always think of the reader and how to bring the reader into the adventure of story. Dialogue is the key here, and this book presents a well-crafted chapter on how to teach students to write dialogue and make characters come alive.

As a writer, the most important thing I do is capturing my story ideas and snippets of language in my writer's notebook. *Absolutely Write!* offers sound advice to teachers of writing and young writers on how to create and keep a writer's notebook.

Tommy Thomason is an accomplished writer and one of America's leading authorities on process writing. Carol York is a practitioner who understands teachers, schools, and young writers. Together, they have created a powerful book that will transform classrooms and the teaching of writing.

I loved this book—and so will you. You'll be a better writer after putting Thomason and York's advice into practice. And as you grow as a writer, so will your student-authors.

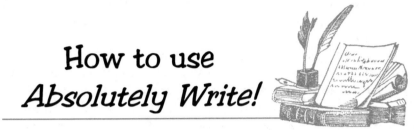

How to use
Absolutely Write!

Novelist Olivia Goldsmith (1996) tells the story of a time God decided to visit the earth:

> Strolling down the road, God encountered a
> sobbing man. "Why are you crying, my son?"
> The man said, "God, I am blind." So God touched him
> and the man could see and was happy.
> As God walked farther he met another crying man and
> asked, "Why are you crying, my son?"
> The man said, "God, I am crippled." So God touched
> him and the man could walk and was happy.
> Farther down the road God met yet a third man crying
> and asked, "Why are you crying, my son?"
> The man said, "God, I'm a writer." And God sat down
> and cried with him.   (p. xiv)

And if writers feel that desire to weep over the difficulties of their craft, how about writing *teachers?* If anything is more difficult than producing a readable piece of prose or poetry, it would have to be teaching others to do it.

If you're a writing teacher, you undoubtedly have those sit-down-and-cry days. You live in a classroom world of high-stakes testing and crowded curriculum and hurry-up school days, and you are expected to produce students who can write across the curriculum for diverse audiences.

You deal with the real world of writing workshop every day, coping with questions like: How do I teach them to write descriptively? How can I move them away from formula leads? How can I help them fall in love with writing itself? How can I illustrate the power of effective voice? How can I help them see how to work dialogue into their pieces? How do I teach expository writing?

And sometimes, truth be told, we have to admit that while we've read the text-book answers to these questions, we're not really sure we understand those answers ourselves. That's where *Absolutely Write!* comes in. This book was written to talk with you, adult to adult, about basic craft elements of writing and to illustrate, from both adult and children's literature, what constitutes an effective lead or an engaging passage of description. And then to illustrate how that craft can be taught in a workshop environment.

Absolutely Write! adds one more key element: involvement experiences that help you experience these craft elements first-hand. If your child couldn't swim and you spent three years taking him to swimming seminars and short courses and having him read books on swimming, would that make him a swimmer? Of course not. You can't learn to swim without getting wet. And you can't become a better writing teacher until you have experienced writing as a writer. Not as a teacher – as a practitioner of the craft yourself. You're probably not the next Jane Yolen, J.K. Rowling, or Jerry Spinelli. But anyone can learn to craft readable, even occasionally elegant, prose and poetry. And then we teach, not from the notes we took at the last Donald Graves seminar, but from our own experience as a writer. That experience, by the way, will enrich more than your classroom; the next time you do sit in a Donald Graves seminar, you'll listen with new ears. You'll hear him as a writer.

Thus this book. Lots of books deal with the topics covered here—basic techniques of effective writing. But what *Absolutely Write!* does is to present these techniques to you as an adult and potential writer yourself, not just as information to pass along to your class.

One last thing: Don't set yourself up for an unfulfilling experience with this book by treating it as just another book to read. It isn't. It's a manual for transforming your writing classroom. Skim the entire book first if you'd like, but then go back and take it chapter by chapter, implementing each craft idea into your classroom—and into your own writing. Your own writing will change; your classroom will change; and yes, *you* will change, too.

So let's get started.

Reference

Goldsmith, O. (1996). *The bestseller.* New York: HarperPaperbacks.

Workshop 1

Getting Started: Anyone Can Write

Your neighbor *insists* his cousin knows someone whose teen-ager returned from Lover's Lane to find a hook caught on his car door. Another friend claims he *actually saw* the television news story about the man who was drugged in a cheap hotel by a body-parts thief who stole his kidneys. A colleague tells you her brother-in-law *really knows* a man who picked up a hitchhiker near a lake but she vanished when he drove her to her destination.

They are called urban myths. People insist they are true, but they are all just legends that help us deal with our realities and cope with our fears.

There are an equal number of writing myths. Though we may at least suspect that the *Man with the Hook* does not exist, we sometimes accept the writing myths without question. And when we do, we find ourselves armed with the excuses we need in order to avoid writing.

Maybe that's you.

You believe you're just not a writer. You weren't born with that talent. You don't write well and you never will. You don't really have anything to say on paper anyway. Or maybe you've tried to write and found that you just weren't inspired to follow through or you were afflicted with a major case of writer's block.

If that's you, get ready for some good news. Every sentence in the previous paragraph is the result of a dirty, rotten lie. Myths, every one of them. Not a single word of truth—not a single valid concept.

And here's the kicker: If you, as a teacher, believe these myths about writing, you'll probably unconsciously transfer these beliefs to your students. (How do *you* think you got them in the first place?)

Rejecting the Myths About Writing

Perhaps in no area of our lives do we blindly accept as true so many misunderstandings. Today, let's look at some of the commonly held writer's myths.

Myth: Writing is a talent. Some have it, some don't. And if you don't . . . just give up on becoming a writer.

Truth: If you can talk, you can write. How do we communicate orally? Do we stop every few words and edit ourselves and examine what we said for its correctness or creativity? No, we just keep talking. If we don't think we communicated well, we keep on verbally revising until we are satisfied with the product.

Writing works the same way. The best speakers are those who do a lot of it before an audience. Most speakers develop their abilities by speaking, just like writers get better by writing. True, there is a talent for writing, and some writers are naturally talented—just like some people are born with a talent for music and perform flawlessly at an early age. But most musicians have learned from other musicians by practicing and performing.

The good news is that writing is a craft—something you can learn, not a talent—something you're good at from birth. When you take your teen to enroll in driver's education, the instructor doesn't ask if the ability to drive runs in your family. The instructor assumes that whether or not the parents can drive, he or she can take a non-driving teen, expose that teen to some principles in class, demonstrate behind a wheel, and then let him or her learn by experience.

The same is true of writing. It's true both for you and the kids in your class—anyone can improve as a writer.

Myth: You must be inspired to produce a really good piece of writing.

Truth: Writers laugh at the idea of inspiration so fondly held by non-writers. One professional put it this way: "I write when I'm inspired. And I see to it that I'm inspired at 9 o'clock every morning."

The idea behind inspiration is that your muse, or the very force of the idea itself, takes over and makes writing easy—almost dictates to you as the ideas and the very words themselves flow effortlessly from your pen.

Hogwash. Most writing is work. On those occasions when you might experience *inspiration,* whatever that is, be grateful for it. But never let a lack of inspiration stop you from writing. If you're not inspired, and the words do not come easily, you might not write if you believe the following myth.

Myth: It's better not to write if you feel you are not producing quality work or giving it your best effort. No writing is better than bad writing.

Truth: If you believe this, we can guarantee one thing about you: You don't write. As teachers, especially, we have been conditioned to "always do your best work." And if we aren't doing our best work, we think, it's better not to write at all.

Nothing could be further from the truth. Many say they would write more if they were better writers. The truth, of course, is that they would be better writers if they wrote more.

That's not to say we should seek to write poorly. Rather, we should realize that the only way to learn to write is to write. Sometimes we will be pleased with what we write; often we won't. But we must keep writing if we are to improve.

"We have to write badly," William Faulkner said, "in order to write well."

Myth: Writer's block affects all writers eventually.

Truth: Writer's block doesn't exist.

Actually, the myth is partly true. All writers experience times "when the well dries up," when it's very difficult to write. But writers keep on writing, even through those times.

All teachers start their careers with starry-eyed optimism. But soon come the days when they don't feel like going to work, when they want desperately to stay at home in bed and not see a student all day. Do they call the office and claim "teacher's block"?

The very idea sounds ludicrous. On such days, you go to school and teach anyway. Learning can and does occur on such days.

What do writers do when they experience writer's block? Here's what writing pro Joel Saltzman (1993) tells his classes:

> What you call writer's block I call *perfectionist's block.* Instead of sitting down and writing something, you worry that your work won't be good enough, or "perfect" enough; or you *start* writing something, but soon give up, convinced it's never going to be the "masterpiece" you'd imagined. One student I know spends 10 percent of his time writing and 90 percent of the time worrying if his work is any good. He doesn't write very much, but he has plenty of time for worrying. (p. 150)

Myth: Be original. Don't copy the style of other people.

Truth: Imitation is one of the best ways to learn writing.

Visit any art gallery and you'll see art students copying the works of the masters. Is that because they someday want to slavishly imitate Monet's style? Not at all. They are learning technique, which they will eventually adapt and apply in their own original paintings.

That's why reading is so important. We need to get the cadence and vocabulary and images of great prose and poetry into our mind's ear through reading and even memorization. As writers, it's good to try occasionally to imitate the style of a writer we like—it's one of the best ways to learn technique. Joan Didion typed the stories of Ernest Hemingway as a young writer to get insight into how the great stylist crafted his sentences. Gay Talese did the same with F. Scott Fitzgerald. John Updike said that writers read, "not to come and judge, but to come and steal."

Myth: People can't write unless they have something to write about.

Truth: You'll never have something to write about until you write.

Many people claim that they will begin to write when they begin to come up with great writing ideas. Of course, they never do, so they never write.

If only they had known the truth: That you begin first to write—as a commitment, as a discipline, developing eventually into a habit. And because you are writing every day, you begin to see the world through writer's eyes. Because you know you will be sitting down each day to write, you begin to think like a writer. You constantly are on the lookout for topics, for dialogue, for an apt turn of phrase, for an image that might be turned into a story or a poem. You don't come up with ideas so you can write ... you commit to writing, and therefore begin to come up with ideas.

· · · · · · · ·

If you have unknowingly bought in to these myths, no wonder you don't write or don't enjoy writing. This book will help you reject the stinking thinking these myths represent and support you as you build positive images of writing into your students.

Writing experiences for teachers

✔ Write how you feel about writing. Even if you hate to write. Tell exactly how you feel about writing, and why you think you feel that way.

✔ Think about the best writing teacher you ever had. Write about him or her. Why was that teacher so good? How did he or she influence you? What characteristics of that person's classroom are you trying to reproduce in your own?

✔ Think of either your worst writing teacher or the worst experience you ever had as a writer. Why was that teacher so bad, or that experience so bad? What lasting effects might it have on you today, your attitudes toward writing, or your classroom?

✔ Complete the following thought: I'd be a better writing teacher if.... This might involve anything you do, anything you say, anything you *are* in the classroom. Even if it looks now like something you could not or would not ever do, go ahead and write about what you think would definitely improve your writing classroom.

Classroom experiences for young writers

If you have fallen prey to any of these writing myths, you know how it can inhibit your growth as a writer. And you don't want that to happen to your students. So what can you do to keep those myths out of your students' writing lives?

The answer is simple: Most of us unconsciously picked up our writing myths from classes that emphasized product over process. They never showed us *how* to generate a writing idea and turn it into text to share with an audience. So the best way to combat the myths is to create a writer-friendly classroom that offers kids lots of chances to write and to take risks in their writing, but also shows them how to implement principles of good writing in the pieces they are working on.

Teachers who do this create a genuine writer's workshop environment in their classes where student writers deal with writing up close and personal on a daily basis. These writers, though they may be young, have been vaccinated against the myths that plague so many adults.

Sally Stephens, a writing resource teacher, bans the myths from her classroom by routinely assessing her students' writing, looking for needs she can address in craft lessons as well as successes she can celebrate. The interested tone of her voice and the smile on her face combine with her comments to let her writers know when they have done well.

She also knows that if her students are to develop independence as writers, they must be allowed to share in the assessment. The criteria for success is no secret! So self-assessment becomes a part of her classroom as students learn about the characteristics of good writing and how to identify them—or the lack of them—in their own pieces.

Charts displaying those characteristics are prominently displayed in her classroom and referred to in craft lessons and in writing and editing conferences. Students use these characteristics of good writing to assess their own writing and the writing of their classmates—and when students know what good writing is and what it looks like on paper, they are better able to produce it themselves. Sally's craft lessons help her students to know *how* to produce the kind of good writing they are studying.

For example, good writing has a logical flow, answering readers' questions as it moves from one idea to the next. But many fourth graders write one sentence after another without stopping to develop the ideas presented. Their stories read like lists. Sally's students were no exception until she taught her "Gizmo" lesson.

Using the predictable workshop structure, Sally let her students know the craft they would be working on in the lesson. They would be stretching their "listy" writing into more effective pieces. She began the lesson by reading an excerpt from Gloria Houston's (1992) *But No Candy,* asking her students to listen with "writers' ears." Following a discussion of the writing, Sally placed a short piece she had written about her dog, Gizmo, on the overhead projector.

The piece listed sentences about Gizmo, but never stayed long enough on any one idea to develop it. Sally selected a *shared writing* strategy[1] to give all the writers in her class the appropriate level of support and increase their opportunity for success. She and her students worked together to revise and stretch the "listy" piece into one that would engage their readers.

Following the shared writing, students selected pieces from their writing folders to revise as they worked independently. Sally conferenced briefly with individuals about the progress of their pieces. For some, this conference was an opportunity to clarify a thought. For others, the conference provided an added bit of support to help the writer over a bump just at the point of need.

This day's workshop ended with students sharing their writing and giving feedback in pairs.

Sally's fourth graders will use this technique again in another piece. She will continue to assess in order to select the focus for future lessons. The predictability of the writers' workshop structure combined with an understanding of the characteristics of effective writing and specific craft lessons provide an environment in her classroom that allows students to succeed as writers. The old writing myths gain no foothold with these students. They're too immersed in writing realities.

Setting up your writer's workshop

Lisa, a first-year teacher, waited until mid-November before she finally approached her colleague across the hall. Her frustration with teaching writing had been growing since the school year started.

It was Friday afternoon and Nancy was packing up to leave the building when Lisa knocked reluctantly on Nancy's open door.

"Can we talk for a few minutes?" she asked tentatively. "It's about writing."

Nancy put down the canvas bag she had packed with books and papers.

"One of my favorite topics. What's on your mind?"

Lisa poured out the frustration: "Writing just isn't working for my kids. I want my students to become competent, confident writers. Like yours. In order for that to happen, I know that I need to create a writer-friendly environment in my classroom. But how do I do that while I manage writing time *and* meet the needs of all my students *and* teach them how to use the writing process *and* help them with grammar and conventions?

"And oh yeah, the state writing test is coming up next spring. I need to be sure my kids are ready. I don't want to bomb this in my first year of teaching."

When Lisa finally stopped for a breath, Nancy said, "Let me tell you about our writer's workshop." Then she shared the instructional model that has allowed teachers throughout the nation to balance the use of process writing with content to be learned and help all writers in the classroom—regardless of achievement level—to grow.

Quite simply, writer's workshop provides a simple, predictable structure that enables the teacher to demonstrate what she wants students to learn to do (the craft lesson), allows time for them to practice while the teacher coaches, and gives young authors a chance to share their writing—a step that is essential to motivation and growth.

How do you implement writer's workshop in your class? First, determine what your writers need. Assessing student writing before you begin workshop allows you to select a teaching point that is needed by most of your writers, one which will keep them growing as writers. This assessment can be accomplished by taking notes as you conference with them about their work in progress and by reading class sets of their writing. You won't have to read every single piece your kids have written in order to inform your instruction. As you implement workshop, you will find that this model gives you in-depth knowledge of what your students can do and what they need to learn.

Plan your craft lesson. Craft lessons (sometimes called mini-lessons) are focused teaching times dealing with one writing competency—like how to improve leads or choose a topic—and based on the literature young writers are familiar with. Here's how to put together your craft lesson:

- Select and share a piece of literature that demonstrates the teaching point.
- Model the teaching point by writing in front of your students, thinking aloud about the decisions you make as a writer.

or

- Share the composition of a piece with your students, focusing on the teaching point. You hold the pen and scribe while the students contribute ideas for the piece. For young students, you may choose to use interactive writing, a form of shared writing. [For a thorough discussion of interactive writing, see McCarrier, Pinnell and Fountas' (2000) *Interactive Writing.*]

Allow students time to write independently or in small groups. This is their time to practice the writing skill or strategy that you just demonstrated. As they write, circulate and conference with individual students about his or her piece. Conference with a few students each day. Decide on a simple recording system, one that works for you; jot down notes as you conference to make sure that everyone gets coaching support from you over a period of time. As students grow, you can introduce peer conferencing.

Let young authors share their writing with an audience. This may be in author's chair, in pairs, or in small groups. The audience/listener(s) respond to the writer by making positive comments, asking questions and offering suggestions to the writer.

Writer's workshop helps create a writer-friendly environment. Teachers using the workshop model teach writing skills and strategies and the conventions of standard written English while supporting their students as they learn to write by writing.

Note

1. Shared writing is when teachers and students collaborate on a piece, with the teacher acting as the scribe (see note on page 5).

References

Houston, G. (1992). *But no candy.* New York: Philomel Books.

McCarrier, A., et. al. (2000) *Interactive writing: How language and literature come together,* K–2. Portsmouth, NH: Heinemann.

Saltzman, J. (1993). *If you can talk, you can write.* New York: Warner Books.

Keeping a Writer's Notebook:
Playing with Prose and Poetry

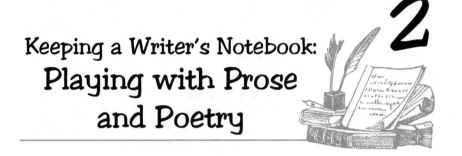

You might have heard a professional basketball player referred to as a "gym rat." That term isn't synonymous with basketball player. In fact, many players aren't, and their coaches wish they were. Pro basketball players spend lots of time warming up for games and playing their games. And they spend hours in practices supervised by their coaches, working on different aspects of team and individual performances. But when practice is over and coaches and players head for their homes, the gym rats stay behind. They are the players who spend extra hours working on free throws or shooting short turnaround jumpers or three-point shots, hundreds of times. They are working on the competencies and skills they know they need to succeed.

Writers learn in the same way. They read books about writing. They read other writers for ideas and examples. They attend workshops and seminars and classes. But it all comes together in daily writing time, working on the skills they need to become better writers.

And lots of writers use a writer's notebook to work on their writing. It's not a journal or a diary, though many entries might well be virtually identical. Instead, a writer's notebook is an opportunity to play with writing and the techniques of writing. Keeping a writer's notebook does not assume a what-do-I-feel-like-writing-about-today approach. Instead, writers look for opportunities to expand their horizons by experimenting with styles and methods and genres. You can use the **Writing experiences for teachers** section of each chapter to get you started using a writer's notebook. They'll jump-start your writer's notebook habit, giving you a topic for each day while reinforcing what you're learning in each of the *Absolutely Write* workshops.

Getting Started with Your Writer's Notebook

✔ First, you need a notebook. Don't go to a bookstore and buy one of those expensive padded-leather journals with the expensive paper and gilt edges. They're beautiful, and that's the problem. You'll think you need to do your best work in them, and you'll want to write neatly. Both are killers when it comes to keeping a writer's notebook. Instead, your only goal is to write. It may occasionally be pretty good; many days, your writing will be pretty bad. But like falling down frequently is a necessary part of learning to walk, bad writing is a necessary part of becoming a writer. Buy the cheap notebook and don't be afraid to cross out, to write in handwriting not even a mother could love, to write with no thought of whether you are producing a piece of any quality at all.

✔ Next, you need to commit to some writing time every day, at least five days a week, or at least on some sort of regular schedule. If 15 minutes a day three days a week is all you can do right now, start there. While you're reading this book, make the **Writing experiences for teachers** exercises a part of your writer's notebook.

✔ Just write. Don't edit. And don't go back and re-read to see if you are improving. Improvement will indeed come, over a period of time. The emphasis for the first few months, though, should just be on writing.

✔ Pay no attention to your internal editor, The Teacher Inside You, who will remind you of every red mark you ever got on a paper, or will bring to mind every unkind comment someone ever made about something you wrote, or will cause you to wonder if you have dangled participles or misspelled words. Those are all issues for later. Right now you are trying to build your self-image as a writer, to get comfortable with the writer's craft, to build fluency in writing. And the only way you do those things is to write. Write playfully. Experiment with words. Try an approach, and if you don't like if after three or four sentences, just start again.

✔ Figure out how long you want to write every day. Make it reasonable for your schedule, and stick to it. When you run out of time, just stop—you don't even have to finish the sentence you're working on. Don't worry about not finishing the paragraph you started or the poem you were writing. You may well want to come back and write more the next day. But maybe not. You don't develop as a writer by finishing a piece; you develop by writing regularly.

✔ Right now, the writing experiences in this book will give you a framework for your writer's notebook. After you finish this book, continue with your writer's notebook. Here are some ideas on what you might want to include:

   • Write letters to the editor of newspapers, magazines, professional journals, etc.

- Write open letters to parents of your children, explaining your approach to writing or reading instruction, or teaching math or social studies, or integrating the arts into the curriculum.

- Start the picture book or chapter book you've always wanted to write. If you are writing 15 minutes a day, write that long every day on the book. Write until you're finished or so sick of it that you want to abandon it and do something else.

- Write poetry. You might look up the formula for a sonnet and try your hand at that complicated rhyme scheme. Or you might try to imitate the poetry of e.e. cummings. Or you may want to write poetry for your children. Or write poetry to be set to music. Maybe you want to pick a content area like history or math or science and write poems to go along with what you are teaching.

- Lots of writers use their writer's notebook to record childhood memories. Every day, write about a different memory: your childhood pet, your best friend in elementary school, physical descriptions of your elementary school teachers, things you were good at and things you weren't, your favorite game as a child, your favorite place to hide as a child, the worst trouble you ever got into, your first paying job, your first kiss, how you learned to drive, your best or worst sports experience. As you write, use the principles and techniques discussed later in this book—the *show, don't tell* principle, strong verbs, engaging leads, dialogue, etc. If you write about the day your mom took you out for your first driving lesson, for instance, you might do that piece purely as dialogue between the two of you. Or it may become a narrative poem. Either way helps you develop as a writer.

✔ Keep everything you do. You may abandon a piece after the bare minimum of time you have promised yourself you'll spend writing every day, silently shaking your head, happy that no one will ever have to see what you just wrote. But two months from now, you get a similar idea and you re-visit this piece, tweak it a little, and come up with something you're proud of.

✔ On the back inside cover of the notebook, keep a list of writing topics that come to you while you are writing about something else. This will happen lots of times—you'll be writing a piece when an idea for another piece will present itself. Quickly turn to your topic list and jot it down, then return to the business at hand. When you stare at your notebook and can't think of anything to write about, flip over to your idea compost heap and pull something out. You're in business.

✔ If you read something you really like, feel free to spend a session copying, not writing. Copy the passage that impressed you into your notebook. And then tomorrow, come back and re-read what you copied the day before. Ask yourself, "Why did I copy that? What impressed me about that paragraph or poem? What did the author do that made it so effective?" In your writer's notebook, answer those questions. Your answer may be a prose paragraph or just a list. The next day, review what you copied one more time, and review your list of why it worked for you. Then, try those same techniques yourself on something you write.

✔ Finally, use your notebook to play with ideas and images that may later play an important part in your writing. Writer Arno Karlen (1993) tells how he uses his writer's notebook:

> My journal, though sometimes personal, is largely a workshop and record of events and ideas. There I collect anecdotes, conversations, and descriptions of faces and voices I encounter. I comment on public events and my reading. I record phrases that seem to have special life or vibrancy, but that have no place in what I'm currently writing. And, of course, I note ideas for articles, stories, and poems that aren't ready to be written. These I leave in the journal to ripen.
>
> A writer's journal isn't like anyone else's. Other people can settle for outpourings to Dear Diary. Not writers. Our journals are where we exercise our imagination and craft, as a dancer works at the bar each day or a musician practices. There, we become our own best teachers (p. 32).

Writing experiences for teachers

Before tomorrow, go to the store and pick up an inexpensive notebook. If you are more comfortable using a computer, that's OK, too. Just be sure that your computer will be available when and where you want to write every day. If you keep your writer's notebook on a computer, establish a folder called Writer's Notebook and save each day's work separately with a filename that includes the date.

Start with these writing experiences about childhood memories:

✔ Write about something you were really good at as a child. Explain as fully as you have time to do.

✔ Write about one time in your childhood when you were really afraid. Why were you afraid? What happened?

✔ Tell about your first paying job. Today's piece might address questions like these: What was it? How did you get it? What did you do? How much did you make? How long did you keep it? What was your biggest adjustment to the world of work? Did you do a good job? What did you learn?

✔ Write about your parents. What kind of people were they? What did they look like? What was important to them? How did they show you how they felt about you? What about them do you try to emulate today? What about them do you hope never shows up in your life?

Classroom experiences for young writers

Sneed Collard's *The Forest in the Clouds* (2000) is open on Robert's desk as he carefully studies the illustration, reads and re-reads the first few pages.

> From east to west the tropical trade winds blow, sucking up moisture like dry, thirsty lungs from the warm Caribbean Sea. After traveling thousands of miles, these warm, wet winds strike land. They rush over the lowlands and then begin to climb. Up and up the winds climb, cooling as they rise higher and higher. As they cool, the moisture in the winds is squeezed out of them.

Then he opens his worn writer's notebook and copies Sneed's words onto his own page. Plagiarism? Not at all.

Robert, a fourth grader in Mr. Johnson's class, is working on a project about ocean life. He knows that for this project he must gather information and write a report, a poem, and an informational or persuasive brochure. Robert is fascinated by the information he has gathered and wants his classmates and others to be interested in his project. So he has turned to informational books that he enjoys in order to check out the craft techniques the authors used.

He has read several of Collard's books and knows that information will be presented in a reader-friendly fashion. So when Mr. Johnson brought the new book into the classroom, Robert grabbed it and headed to his seat to settle in for a good read. Right away he noticed the verbs that made him feel the tropical winds described. Just last week Mr. Johnson and Robert had talked about the importance of verbs in writing. Robert knew this was an area in his own writing that he wanted to improve. So he decided to copy a sample from the book and try to write about ocean life using carefully chosen verbs to make his own readers picture what he wanted them to see. With the cap of the highlighter pen in his mouth, he carefully highlighted the verbs to remind himself why he copied this passage.

Mr. Johnson teaches his students to use their writer's notebooks to help them grow as writers. So while Robert is copying another writer's work into his writer's notebook, Hannah and Yesenia are trying out different poetry forms in theirs. Yesenia is trying her hand with sensory poems about whales, her chosen ocean life topic. Hannah has decided to experiment with cinquains about dolphins. They are both comfortable playing with poetry forms in their notebooks. This is where they can play with words and take risks. Risks that will eventually lead to the poetry they will write, revise and publish as part of their project.

Next door, Miss Peeple's students are also working on their ocean life projects. Eric and Ian are comparing their research notes on stingrays when Eric is reminded of an incident the previous summer on his family's beach vacation. He and his little brother had been playing in the surf when they wandered into a school of rays. He was proud of the way he quickly thought to teach his little brother to do the "stingray shuffle" to avoid the painful sting of the rays. Thinking that this might be a good idea for a future piece, he turns to the pocket in the back of his writer's notebook, where he keeps a list of ideas for writing. He quickly adds this idea to the list and mentions it to Ian as they return to their research notes and begin to plan their brochure about stingrays.

Miss Peeple's students are adept at keeping a list of writing ideas in their notebooks because they see her keep such a list. She frequently gets an idea for a future piece during class. When this happens she adds the idea to her writer's notebook or to a list prominently displayed in the classroom. Another day, when she models for students, she will turn to the list for a topic to write about. This shows the young writers the value of keeping such a list for days when they want to lament, "I can't think of anything to write about!"

Problem solved. Check the list in your writer's notebook.

Both Miss Peeples and Mr. Johnson encourage their students to use their writer's notebook to write letters about issues of concern to them. One burning issue with their fourth and fifth grade students is the proposal to add an extra 45 minutes to the school day and several days to the school year. Several of their students write letters of total opposition while others write in support of the extra time but only if they would be allowed to choose the activity for the extra time. Because all the students feel strongly about this issue, they write intensely to achieve their purpose. While they are free to express their opinions in these letters, it is not the opinions that are important. It is the growth that occurs as these students write to express those opinions that is important.

These teachers, like many others, use writer's notebooks in their classrooms to help their students to be more comfortable with different writing craft techniques, to build fluency and to see themselves as writers. Their students write about their observations of both ordinary and extraordinary events. They write descriptions, try out various types of writing, collect examples of other writers' work that they admire, or play around with word choice. Keeping a writer's notebook is one more strategy that these teachers use to help their students meet their goal to become fluent, effective writers.

References

Collard, S. (2000). *The forest in the clouds.* Watertown, MA: Charlesbridge Publishing.

Karlen, A. (1993). "Journal-ism made easy," *Writer's Digest,* February 1993.

Freewriting:
Silencing Our Internal Editors

If you hear voices in your head, you're probably concerned and may even be in therapy. But if you only hear them when you write, you're probably not worried. In fact, you probably accept them as a normal part of the writing process.

They aren't.

Those voices are left over from every time anyone embarrassed you by criticizing your writing in public, or red-penciling a piece you were proud of, or telling you that your piece was bad or you were no writer. You can barely remember the names of your tenth grade English teacher or your freshman composition professor, but their voices haunt your subconscious mind whenever you write.

And what do the voices say?

> "That's no good."
> "You could have done better."
> "Is that really your best work?"
> "You should be glad nobody can see this."

The result? We avoid writing. Or we're unwilling to take chances. Or we just dislike writing (as we typically dislike *anything* we think we're no good at) and we stop.

So how do we make the voices go away, so we can just write?

The Essentials of Freewriting

One technique a lot of writers use to clear the cobwebs and stimulate their creativity and turn off the negative voices is freewriting. The technique is simple: Just write. Put pen to paper and get black on white for 10 minutes or so. Write anything. It doesn't have to be good. It doesn't even have to be coherent. Don't stop for anything. Don't stop to re-read or revise or fix anything or even cross something out. If you can't think of a word you need, either describe the concept as best you can in other words or write "I can't think of the word I'm looking for here."

What if you get stuck for the next idea? You write "I'm stuck for the next idea" as many times as necessary until the next idea comes to you, and then you move on. Whatever, you never stop writing until your pre-determined time limit is up.

Teachers sometimes find freewriting more threatening than other people. After all, it's full of incoherent statements, errors, sloppiness, and mindless repetition. It's almost never good writing, though at times it does contain some good writing or at least the germs of ideas that can be turned into good writing. But why would you write with no concern for the very concepts we try to teach as good writing?

Simple. Because it helps us to get comfortable with the writing process. When we were learning to speak, our parents let us make mistakes as a child. If you told your parents "Me want cookie," they didn't talk to you about nominative pronouns in subject positions and the importance of articles. They gave you a cookie. And they didn't worry that you'd off to college still saying "Me want...." They understood that speaking is a process learned over a period of time through meaningful interactions.

Then, when you got to school and began to learn to write, the *error hunt* began. Writing was seen as a pretext to point out mistakes.

We still frequently "talk out" problems. We do that because we know we can just say what's on our mind without editing it, letting ideas flow freely. We're not concerned with saying the right thing, just getting our ideas out. And that stimulates our creativity. Talking out problems lets us turn off our editor.

And that's what happens when we freewrite. Peter Elbow (1973) explains how it works:

> Editing, *in itself,* is not the problem. Editing is usually necessary if we want to end up with something satisfactory. The problem is that editing goes on *at the same time* as producing. The editor is, as it were, constantly looking over the shoulder of the producer and constantly fiddling with what he's doing while he's in the middle of trying to do it. No wonder the producer gets nervous, jumpy, inhibited, and finally can't be coherent. It's an unnecessary burden to try to think of words and also worry at the same time whether they're the right words. (p. 5)

Freewriting gets rid of that unnecessary burden. And in the process, you'll find yourself coming up with ideas you can develop later and with entire sections of your freewrite that can be revised and polished and edited into a piece you can be proud of.

So what does it accomplish?

- *Freewriting frequently helps you find your writer's voice because you are writing without constraints.*
- *It's a compost pile of ideas for later pieces.*

- ***It sets you free to write without constantly evaluating what you do.*** Good writers know that writing comes first, that revision and editing come later. If we try to edit during the writing process we inhibit our writing. Many teachers will teach that concept in writing workshop but not apply it in their own writing—and thus not really understand it.

- ***Freewriting stimulates your creativity because it encourages the free flow of ideas.*** The more you do it, the better you'll get. It will feel unnatural at first, maybe even downright dangerous to your writing ability. But go ahead and write—you'll become more adept at freewriting the more often you do it.

  Some writers freewrite several times a week, some only when they feel they need to break out of a writer's rut, and some writers never freewrite at all. We have included it as a technique that many writers—especially writers who aren't that comfortable with the writing process—find helpful.

The **Writing experiences for teachers** section of this chapter gives you the opportunity to do two kinds of freewriting in your writer's notebook. The first is the traditional freewriting, where you just put pen to paper and begin to write, following only your own train of thought. The second kind is a focused freewrite, in which you freewrite on a topic by limiting your thinking to that controlling idea.

Writing experiences for teachers

✔ Time to try it yourself. Write with a clock nearby, so you can time out ten minutes. When you put pen to paper, don't stop. Write about whatever goes through your mind. If all you can think of is how stupid you consider freewriting to be, write about that. Just don't stop until your ten minutes is up.

✔ So how was it yesterday? Today, do the same thing, again for ten minutes.

✔ Do a focused freewrite. The topic is simply "Teaching." Beginning with that concept, start writing and continue for ten minutes.

✔ Try this topic: "If I Were to Write a Book, I'd Write About...." Write for ten minutes.

Classroom experiences for young writers

Phil Bailey has seen the look many times before on the faces of his fifth graders early in the school year when he begins writing workshop like this:

> All right, young writers, today we're going to freewrite. That means you put your pencil down on the paper and start writing. Just whatever comes to mind. You never look back. And you won't stop writing for 10 minutes. Don't worry about grammar or spell-

ing or punctuation or even making sense. Just put down any idea
that comes to your mind about anything. You may write about lots
of different things in your ten minutes. That's OK. The object of
freewriting is to let your ideas flow.

Most of Phil's writers come from very structured writing environments where
correctness and planning were emphasized over fluency. They frequently stare at
their writer's notebooks for a long time, waiting for just the right words to appear
magically in their heads. So he uses freewriting early in the year to get them
accustomed to thinking on paper.

When he explains freewriting the first time, he can see the pained expressions
on faces. This is a totally different approach to writing. But it's not long before his
fifth graders are busily hunkered over their notebooks, pencils flying across the
paper, enjoying their new freedom.[1]

Phil's experience in his suburban Dallas middle school mirrors that of Kyle
Gonzalez, a middle school teacher in Orlando, Florida. Kyle wrote about one
freewriting experience in her book *There's Room for Me Here* (1998). Alex had
just returned to Kyle's class after being suspended from school for ten days. He
wasn't happy to be back in class, and his complaining attitude soon spread to
others in the class. Before long, many students were voicing their complaints
about the school and their teachers. Kyle decided it was time for freewriting:

"Okay, it's time to get some of this negativity out," I announced.
"You need to get out a piece of paper and something to write
with." After a great deal of shuffling around, lots of complaining,
and much borrowing of paper and pens, we were finally ready to
write.

"Let's take three minutes and get what we're feeling out on
paper. I just want us to get our thoughts down—how we're feeling
about school or what we would rather be doing right now. Remember, this is a freewrite. I don't care about spelling or punctuation at the moment. Ready? Let's write."

The students were familiar with freewrites; it's a tool I use often
in class as a way to respond to something we've read or a problem we're having. I write along with the students, stopping only
briefly to urge on the stragglers. After the three minutes were up,
several students volunteered to share their writing, Alex among
them. I was shocked. His writing was not only the longest piece
he had ever completed, it also had voice and logic.... (p. 96)

Freewriting deals effectively with the old student complaint, "I don't have anything to write about!" And what teacher hasn't seen this same student 15 minutes
later on the playground talking nonstop about his life, his pets, his sports, his
musical interests, his parents, his friends, his hobbies, a recent movie or TV show,
and so on. Obviously, the student had lots of interests—lots to write about. He
had something to say; he just didn't know it. Freewriting is an unstructured, non-
threatening, free association mind search. Little League players might relate to it

as being the same as hitting balls in a batting cage. No one complains if you swing and miss. You're not trying to advance a runner. You're just there to practice, to try variations on your swing, to get used to the idea of swinging a bat and hitting a ball. Freewriting does the same thing with writing. Your goal is to overcome the fear of a blank page and to get in touch with the writing ideas inside you.

Besides just having students put pencil to paper and write, there are other ways to use freewriting in class:

- **Freewrite to pictures:** Show a picture postcard or magazine photo and give students a question on which they can freewrite. Try questions like these: How do you feel as you look at the picture? What is happening in this picture? What would you do if you were in this picture? What happened just before this picture was taken? How would you describe this picture to a blind person?

- **Freewrite creative lists:** This type of freewriting gives young writers an opportunity to brainstorm. Have them list as many things as they can that are sticky, that are scary, that crunch, that melt, that make loud noises, and the like. After a creative listing freewriting, discuss possible writing topics that came up.

- **Freewrite from sentence starters:** You give them an unfinished sentence and let them complete it and write as many additional sentences that extend their meaning as they can during the freewriting period. You might try sentences like these:

  ✔ One thing that really makes me mad is....

  ✔ One thing that really worries me is....

  ✔ I can't wait until I am old enough to....

  ✔ Sometimes I am as happy as....

  ✔ If money were no object, I would....

  ✔ If our school did away with grades, I think students would...

- **Freewrite creative stories:** There are lots of ways to let young writers play with story structure. You may invent a character and let the students give that character a problem. Then let students freewrite how the character deals with the problem. Or read a part of a well-known fairy tale, like *Cinderella.* Then give them a few minutes to come up with their own alternate ending.

- **Freewrite creative responses to questions you supply:** Since there are no right-or-wrong answers here, students can just write whatever comes to mind. You may try questions like these:

  ✔ How would a bull feel in a bullfight?

  ✔ How would a baseball/football/soccer ball/hockey puck feel during a game?

✔ Which is slower—red or blue? Why?

✔ Explain orange.

✔ You are a statue where pigeons roost. How do you feel?

✔ Which is better—Coke or Pepsi? Why?

Follow up freewriting sessions with sharing opportunities. Let students read a sentence they especially liked in their writing. Let them share an idea they got while writing which they would like to develop during writing workshop. The sharing will show young writers how ideas develop during the composition process. They will benefit from their own freewriting and from the the work of others. Rare is the freewriting session when writers do not add several items to their list of potential future writing topics in their writing folder.

Note

1. Some teachers worry about the "anything goes" atmosphere of freewriting, fearing that it produces sloppy work habits and compromises our classroom commitment to quality work. Freewriting guru Peter Elbow (1973) addresses that concern in *Writing Without Teachers:*

> In a sense I'm saying, "Yes, freewriting invites you to write garbage, but it's good for you." But this isn't the whole story. Freewriting isn't just therapeutic garbage. It's also a way to produce bits of writing that are genuinely *better* than usual: less random, more coherent, more highly organized.
>
> It boils down to something very simple. If you do freewriting regularly, much or most of it will be far inferior to what you can produce through care and rewriting. But the good bits will be much better than anything else you can produce by any other method. (pp. 8–9)

References

Allen, J. and Gonzalez, K. 1998. *There's room for me here: Literacy workshop in the middle school.* York, Maine: Stenhouse.

Elbow, P. 1973. *Writing without teachers.* New York: Oxford University Press.

Show, Don't Tell: Painting Pictures with Words

You may still remember one of your former writing teachers telling you, "You need to elaborate."

What that writing teacher meant was that you needed to add detail to make your piece come to life, to help readers picture your setting in their mind's eye. That may be what your teacher *meant*; what we often *heard* was that we needed to add more words, especially adjectives, to make the piece longer.

So our paragraphs grew from three sentences to seven. But since our goal was only adding verbiage, we never saw real improvement.

What our teachers *should* have been telling us was the old writer's maxim: Show, don't tell. Or as Mark Twain put it, "Don't say the old lady screamed. Bring her on the stage and make her scream." Readers love to watch a story happening in their minds. We accomplish this by writing visually, so that the reader becomes an observer.

Pulling Readers Into Text

Suppose we asked a writer to tell an important childhood memory. The writer may produce a piece like this:

> The first memory I have is of picking cotton with my mother. I would ride the cotton sack she pulled behind her when she picked. Those were wonderful times of togetherness for us. We were poor then, but my mother would do all sorts of things that helped me feel important and loved.

The writer *tells* the reader about his favorite memory. But readers are not involved because they cannot picture the scene. The answer is not to elaborate.

Rather, writers need to use sensory detail—sights, sounds, tastes, smells, feelings—that put readers on the scene as observers.

Read Rick Bragg's (1997) description of the same memory in his book *All Over But the Shoutin':*

> The first memory I have is of a tall blond woman who drags a canvas cotton sack along an undulating row of rust-colored ground, through a field that seems to reach into the back forty of forever. I remember the sound it makes as it slides between the chest-high stalks that are so deeply, darkly green they look almost black, and the smell of kicked-up dust, and sweat. The tall woman is wearing a man's britches and a man's old straw hat, and now and then she looks back over her shoulder to smile at the three-year-old boy whose hair is almost as purely white as the bolls she picks, who rides the back of the six-foot-long sack like a magic carpet.
>
> It is my first memory, and the best. It is sweeter than the recollection I have of the time she sat me down in the middle of a wild strawberry patch and let me eat my way out again, richer than all the times she took me swimming in jade-colored streams and threw a big rock in the water to run off the water moccasins. It is even stronger than the time she scraped together money for my high school class ring, even though her toes poked out of her old sneakers and she was wearing clothes from the Salvation Army bin in the parking lot of the A&P. It was not real gold, that ring, just some kind of fake, shiny metal crowned with a lump of red glass, but I was proud of it. I was the first member of my family to have one, and if the sunlight caught it just right, it looked almost real. (pp. 23–24).

Take a minute to re-read Bragg's cotton-patch memory. Note the descriptions of the field, of himself, of his mother. And notice that he never says that his mother loved him or that they had a special bond between them, but we know that is true by the memories he shares.

Will Rogers said that people's minds are changed not through argument, but through observation. So writers put their readers in a position to observe. Gloria Houston (1992), writing about a childhood experience of eating a Hershey bar during a time when candy was in short supply, actually makes your mouth water for chocolate. Look at how she does it:

> If the weather was nice, before she ate her candy bar, Lee would climb to her secret place high in the hickory tree Daddy had planted in the sideyard. When she was safely wedged in where the branches of the tree formed a seat, Lee took the Hershey bar out of her pocket. First, she sniffed the chocolate through the brown and silver paper. Nothing else in the world ever smelled so good. Then she slowly took off the wrapper and smoothed it on her knees. Finally she unfolded the white paper and ate the little

squares one at a time, letting the chocolate melt on her tongue. To Lee, the taste of that chocolate bar was the best thing in the world. (p. 6).

Gloria Houston does not *tell* the reader how delicious the candy is. She *shows* how she ate it, using sensory details that ring true for everyone who ever ate a Hershey bar. Look at the techniques of showing that she used:

- *She gives you a sense of place:* She doesn't say Lee climbed the tree. We know that the place in the tree she climbed to was a "secret" place, probably meaning it was hidden from plain view, obviously a place she climbed often in order to be alone. We know the secret place was formed by branches that came together to provide a seat for her. We know the secret place was high in the tree. We know it was a hickory tree, planted by her father. We know the tree was in the sideyard of her house. We know that when she settled into the secret place, she "wedged" herself in—what a vivid mental picture we can form of Lee climbing the tree and preparing to enjoy her candy!

- *She doesn't characterize the action; she describes it in a narration, moment by moment:* She doesn't just say she opened the candy and ate it and enjoyed it. We know that she had climbed the tree with the Hershey bar in her pocket. Immediately after she wedged herself into her seat, she pulled the candy out of her pocket and sniffed it—before she even took the paper off. The author helps you picture the scene by reminding you that Hershey's is wrapped in brown and silver paper. We follow Lee as she unwraps the candy and smooths it on her knees. At no point does the author say: "It had been so long since Lee ate candy that she wanted to delay her first bite, so she took her time preparing to eat." That's telling. Instead, she conveys the same information, but she does it by taking you, action by action, through Lee's preparations to eat. And if you're a Hershey's lover, you're probably subconsciously thinking, "So hurry up and eat it, Lee!" The author wants to show you the importance of this event in Lee's life by showing you both the anticipation and enjoyment she felt in eating the Hershey bar.

Even poetry can honor the show, don't tell principle. We frequently see poetry as expressing the great universals like love or hate or honor or fear. But think of Edgar Allan Poe's *The Raven* or Robert Frost's *Stopping By Woods on a Snowy Evening.* The first poem immediately gives you an image of a somber 19th century drawing room, the second of a country scene in snowy New England. Why do you have those images? Because even if you don't have the poems memorized, the poets *showed* you such strong visual images in their writing that you still remember the setting of the poems. Here's a poem most teachers will relate to, written by Brod Bagert (1999). The topic is the frustration teachers feel over those "impossible" kids who nonetheless never miss a day of school—and thus never miss an opportunity to present problems in the classroom. That's what the poem is about, but notice how the poet paints a visual image that helps you picture the kid, picture the situations, and even relate to the teacher's frustrations.

Perfect Attendance

By Brod Bagert

> There was a child,
> One of twenty-seven,
> And this child never once sat still,
> Never once behaved nicely,
> And he never paid attention.
> He talked, teased,
> Played, piddled,
> argued and annoyed every creature
> With whom he came into contact,
> And he never missed a day of school!
>
> Andrew Barneby Grimes.
> Last year's Perfect Attendance Award recipient.
>
> Strep throat?
> Andrew came to school.
>
> Eighteen inches of snow?
> Andrew came to school.
>
> A terrorist attack at the mall?
> Andrew came to school.
>
> And I am not surprised.
> You see, Andrew's got a mamma,
> And his mamma ain't no fool.
> When you got a kid like Andrew...?
> You *make* him go to school. (p. 14)

This poem works so well because of all the vivid word pictures the poet gives you. You know how many children in Andrew's classroom (27). The poet could have *told* you that Andrew was unruly and presented a number of behavior problems. Instead, he *showed* you Andrew's behavior in three phrases: We know he never sat still, never behaved nicely, and never paid attention. Not content with that, he drills the point home in a list of action verbs that nail down Andrew's misdeeds. He talked, teased, played, piddled, argued, and annoyed.

Brod Bagert draws us into this poem with his descriptions of Andrew's behavior, then of his faithfulness in attendance. He could have gone from the stanza about Andrew's award to the last stanza. After all, we already know Andrew never missed a day, so why add the types of situations that might cause other kids to miss, but not this one? Because this reinforces the idea that no matter what might happen, even natural or man-made catastrophes, this kid would be in school. The stanza about the award *tells* us this kid was a faithful attender. The next three stanzas (strep throat, snow, mall terrorists) *show* us the extent of that attendance faithfulness, setting up the humorous observation about Andrew's mother in the last stanza.

Is descriptive, visual writing more difficult than dull and lifeless writing? Not at all. In fact, it's easier because it's not abstract. Would you rather write about a mother's love or the time your mother didn't buy a winter coat she needed so you could have the trumpet you needed for band? Would you rather write about "giving your all" in sports or tell about the time you batted in the bottom of the ninth with two out, one runner on base, and your team behind by a run?

As you develop the ability to write visually, you will actually begin to see your life as a writer does, noticing the colors and textures and smells that surround you every day. Nancie Aronie (1998) explains that writers even think of the mundane chore of clothes-packing in a different way:

> Anyone packs a suitcase. Anyone packs two T-shirts, one dress, one pair of jeans, one bathing suit, one pair of shoes, one pair of sneaks. The writer packs the white Donna Karan turtleneck and the navy blue rayon mesh long-sleeve Polo number, the faded-to-perfection *501 Levi's* that you "traded" (stole from) Billy Martinelli when you slept over and found they fit perfectly, the Norma Kamali jade green and black pinstripe bikini with the gold buttons up the side, the black espadrilles with the silver grosgrain ribbons, and the pink high-top Reeboks. Generalizations are boring; rich descriptions are compelling. (p. 139)

The ***Writing experiences for teachers*** section of this chapter will help you develop the ability to both think and write visually for your readers.

Writing experiences for teachers

✔ Think about your childhood pet or some other animal you have known well in your life. Write down several behavioral characteristics of that pet—like playful, mischievous, friendly, etc. Now pick one of those characteristics and describe your pet in such a way that the reader will know your pet had that characteristic, but without using the name of that characteristic. For example, if your dog Fido was playful, tell a story about Fido or tell what Fido would typically do in such a way that will help the reader know Fido is playful, without ever mentioning that word. After you write—and *only* after you finish—read the quoted paragraph below for an example of how Beverly Cleary (1964) did the same thing in describing Ribsy the dog in the book by the same name.

> Henry Huggins' dog Ribsy was a plain ordinary city dog, the kind of dog that strangers usually called Mutt or Pooch. They always called him this in a friendly way, because Ribsy was a friendly dog. He followed Henry and his friends to school. He kept the mailman company. He wagged his tail at the milkman, who always stopped to pet him. People liked Ribsy, and Ribsy liked people. Ribsy was what you might call a well-adjusted dog. (p. 7)

✔ Write about your best memory from childhood. And write it visually. Review Rick Bragg's piece on p. 22 before you begin to write.

✔ Let's work on improving some sentences. Make the *tells* into *shows*. You'll have to add information, so feel free to make it up.

Here's an example:

Tells: Sarah awoke to a noise in her kitchen. She was terrified out of her mind.

Shows: The sound of glass breaking in Sarah's kitchen woke her up. She froze and listened. She could hear the sound of footsteps on the broken glass. Blood pounded in her head as her mind raced through the possibilities of what she could do about the intruder in her home. Sweat washed over her body in waves.

> Now you do these, adding whatever information you think will help the reader picture the scene and situation. Each scenario tells you about an emotion our heroine Sarah feels. Instead, show that emotion. Several sentences should be sufficient for each.

Tells: Sarah wondered if her old boyfriend would be at their 10-year class reunion. And then she saw him standing there by the punchbowl. All her old feelings for him came flooding over her. She froze.

Shows:

Tells: The PTA president introduced Sarah to give the welcome. She was so afraid of public speaking and dreaded the 10-minute address she would have to give.

Shows:

Tells: Sarah loved the ocean. The sound of the waves made her feel at peace.

Shows:

✔ List a few character qualities you think people should have. Then go back and, beside each quality, write the name of someone who has that quality. Then pick one quality and name and write how you know that person exemplifies that quality. For instance, if you say John has patience, tell about a time when John showed patience in the face of adverse circumstances. You will probably have a short narrative. Include dialogue if appropriate and write it descriptively. And finally, don't use the name of the character quality in your narrative. In other words, don't say John has patience; just tell your story in such a compelling way that any reader would be forced to conclude that he did. You're not going to *tell* a reader that John is patient; you want to *show* the reader.

Classroom experiences for young writers

Gloria stood a long time in the hall after school, reading a display of pieces written by the fifth graders in her colleague Jerry's class. She was drawn to the quality of the writing, but at first she couldn't put her finger on just what distinguished the writing of Jerry's young authors. Then she realized what it was: These fifth graders seemed to have a writing maturity far beyond their years because they were learning to paint word pictures in their writing—to show, not tell.

She was still reading the student pieces when Jerry came out of his classroom.

"OK," she said, "tell me how you do it. Your kids seem to know how to pull readers into their writing through their use of description. I've seen much older writers who can't use the techniques your students do. And I'll bet that explains your great writing scores on the state test, too. What's your secret?"

Jerry suggested they sit down over a soft drink in the lounge. During the next few minutes, he shared some simple ways of teaching his fifth graders to think visually. Gloria was excited to see how workable Jerry's strategies were.

Jerry explained that he thought much of his success began with showing his writers how their favorite writers used this technique all the time. Jerry knew that many of his students had seen the movie *The Perfect Storm*. So he brought the book upon which the movie was based to class and read sections to them. They remembered sitting glued to their theater seats as the sailors fought the storm in their small fishing boat. Obviously, the filmmaker had the techniques of computer graphics, excellent actors, and location shooting to involve the reader. But the writer, Sebastian Junger (1997), had to do the same thing with words.

Jerry also brought a VCR tape of the movie to class. He showed only the first couple of minutes, where the moviemaker showed location scenes from Gloucester, Massachusetts. Then he read how Junger did the same thing with words:

> A soft rain slips down through the trees and the smell of the ocean is so strong that it can almost be licked off the air. Trucks rumble along Rogers Street and men in t-shirts stained with fishblood shout to each other from the decks of boats. Beneath them the ocean swells up against the black pilings and sucks back down to the barnacles. Beer cans and old pieces of styrofoam rise and fall and pools of spilled diesel fuel undulate like huge iridescent jellyfish. The boats rock and creak against the ropes and seagulls complain and hunker down and complain some more. (p. 3)

What Jerry did with *The Perfect Storm* was a strategy he used every day—taking a piece of writing his students enjoyed and sharing the process behind the product, how the writer had constructed the parts they enjoyed best. Jerry shared good writing along a continuum from examples written by his own young writers to works of children's literature to the works of adult authors in books and magazines. Sometimes, instead of sharing what the author had written, Jerry would reduce the piece to a fact sheet or a story and let his writers have a chance to produce a paragraph or so based on what he had shared. Then he would show them what the professional had produced with the same input. We used a similar strategy with Rick Bragg's childhood memory cited at the beginning of this chapter.

Gloria was eager to try Jerry's strategies. Teachers working together to refine their classroom practice plays a key part in the success of Gloria and Jerry's school. They are members of a faculty involved in staff development that includes peer coaching (Joyce and Showers, 1988). Teachers frequently visit each other's classrooms to observe specific lessons and then get together to discuss the experience. These observations, along with the discussions and reflections, help teachers to focus on refining their professional practices and have become a routine part of the school's culture. So, it was only natural for Jerry to invite Gloria to his class for the next writer's workshop *show, not tell* mini-lesson.

Prior to the observation, Jerry told Gloria that he wanted to let the students play with the *show, don't tell* principle in quick classroom exercises—just to practice the technique without having to produce a longer piece of writing. As Gloria settled into a chair on one side of the room, Jerry wrote on the board: "Jamie's neighbor doesn't like kids." He talked with them, explaining how that tells, but it doesn't show and began to write and model for them using visual language to give the same information, thinking aloud as he wrote to enable his students to hear and understand the writing decisions he made.

Following the mini-lesson, Jerry gave his students the opportunity to practice on their own while he circulated to conference with individual writers. As he stopped to conference with Eli, he smiled. Eli had written: "Whenever kids are playing near Jamie's neighbor's yard, he throws open his door, stomps out onto his porch, and threatens to call the police because they are disturbing him."

Jerry complimented Eli, a student new to his class, for writing that provided a visual picture that would remain in the minds of readers.

After school Jerry and Gloria met again in his classroom to talk about this lesson and other techniques that they could use to help students paint pictures with words. During the next few weeks, they observed each other as they taught using these techniques and got together afterwards to talk about their teaching and their students' writing. Gloria and Jerry's enthusiasm, as well as their students' vivid writing, soon brought other teachers into the conversations.

Their group devised still more strategies to help students paint word pictures in prose and poetry. Some of their techniques included:

✔ Use pictures to produce visual writing. Bring in postcard scenes or pictures from magazines. Let young writers assume that they are writing a story that happened in one of the places pictured and let them describe what they see in the photograph because they want their readers to be able to picture it. Make a color photocopy of some of the pictures so that two or more students are working on some at the same time. Then compare their descriptions.

✔ Collect great examples of visual writing. When students bring in an example (keep them short, preferably only a paragraph or so), let them read their example and share how the writer used the *show, don't tell* principle. Photocopy those examples and add them to a class book of great visual writing. Keep it in a loose-leaf binder because you will want to re-arrange and re-categorize your examples as the book grows. You will probably end up with examples of descriptive writing under subject-division headings like description of places, description of people, description of things, even descriptive poetry. This keeps visual writing, and its techniques, on the "front burner" of your young writers—and thus they are more likely to use what they have learned when they write.

But perhaps more important than sharing new strategies, Jerry and Gloria had helped to form a community of writing teachers, a group that shared successes and failures and supported each other as they sought more effective ways to help students develop as writers.

References

Aronie, N. (1998). *Writing from the heart: Tapping the power of your inner voice.* New York: Hyperion.

Bagert, B. (1999). *Rainbows, head lice, and pea-green tile: Poems in the voice of the classroom teacher.* Gainesville, FL: Maupin House.

Bragg, R. (1997). *All over but the shoutin'.* New York: Pantheon.

Cleary, B. (1964). *Ribsy.* New York: Dell.

Houston, G. (1992). *But no candy.* New York: Philomel Books.

Joyce, B. and Showers, B. (1988). *Student achievement through staff development.* New York: Longman.

Junger, S. (1997). *The perfect storm.* New York: HarperCollins.

The Power of Verbs: Transforming Lifeless Prose

Find a piece of writing you really like and you'll probably also find strong active verbs. When novice writers think about revision, they frequently consider changes in adverbs and adjectives. Experienced writers begin by looking at verbs.

Verbs are strongest when they are both concrete and precise, when they express real action. A sign writer at the San Diego Zoo who clearly understood the power of specific verbs wrote this warning:

> Please do not annoy, torment, pester, plague, molest, worry, badger, harry, harass, heckle, persecute, irk, bullyrag, vex, disquiet, grate, beset, bother, tease, nettle, tantalize, or ruffle the animals.

Looking for the Right Verb

In terms of their interest for readers, verbs can be classified from the weakest to the strongest:

- Being (the weakest)
- Being done to
- Thinking or feeling
- Saying
- Doing (the strongest)

Here's how they might look in a piece of writing, again beginning with the weakest and moving to the strongest:

- Sarah was upset.
- Sarah was being made upset by her principal.

- Sarah thought her principal was unfair.
- "He's unfair!" Sarah sobbed to her friend.
- Sarah wept as she explained how her principal had turned down her request to attend the workshop.

Sometimes writers will settle for a weak verb but add an adverb to strengthen it, like *I am absolutely and totally unsure of that answer* instead of *I question (or doubt) that answer.* Adverbs are sometimes the enemies of good writing, because they allow us to modify or qualify a weak verb instead of finding the stronger, more descriptive verb. Look at these examples of verb/adverb combinations that could have been improved by stronger verbs:

> touched lovingly—caressed
> moved suspiciously—sneaked
> thought carefully—deliberated or pondered
> held tightly—grasped
> wanted badly—craved.

Also, we sometimes add unneeded words to a verb phrase, like:

> "to become healthy" instead of "to recover"
> "to take a fall" instead of "to trip" or "to fall"
> "to have a suspicion" instead of "to suspect"
> "to make a decision" instead of "to decide"
> "to make use of" instead of "to use."

So do writers always consciously look for exactly the right verb as they write? The good news is that the more you write and the more sensitive you become to verb choice, the more natural your verb selection will become. But the point isn't whether you always choose the best verb when you write. Rather, are verbs one of the first things you look at when you return to revise a piece? And are you becoming sensitive to verb choice in what you read?

Children love Bill Martin Jr.'s (1993) fanciful Halloween story, *Old Devil Wind.* And what makes this story so engaging? Great verbs. Look at this excerpt (the authors have italicized some of Martin's energetic verbs):

> Witch said,
> "Owl, why do you hoot?"
> Owl said,
> "It is a dark and stormy night.
> Ghost *wails*
> Stool *thumps*
> Broom *swishes*
> Candle *flickers*
> Fire *smokes*
> Window *rattles*

Floor *creaks*
Door *slams*
and so I *hoot*."
Witch said,
"Then I shall *fly* around the house."

Carolyn Lesser's (1997) *Storm on the Desert* illustrates the effect of powerful verbs. Her book tells about a day in the life of the desert and its animal life. Lesser has obviously chosen her verbs carefully to give readers a vivid mental picture of the desert creatures (again, note the power of the italicized verbs).

A shadow *slinks*
From a thicket of mesquite.
The coyote *stretches and howls*
To the wisp of the moon.
He *trots,* looking for water,
But finds only cracked earth.
He *sits.*
He *waits.*

A cactus wren's raucous call
Awakens the desert.
Startled bats *swoosh* into caves.
Scorpions *scuttle* under sticks.

Reading great stylists like Martin and Lesser reminds us that verbs are important to compelling writing. Sometimes first drafts don't contain those great verb choices, but when good writers revise, they look for lazy verbs. The first draft might have had a character look out a window. In revision, that becomes stare or gaze or peer or gawk. In the first draft, the character might have walked nervously around the room. In revision, she paces. In the first draft, she ate her lunch quickly. In revision, she wolfed down her food.

As you read and write this week, pay attention to verbs. They are the primary source of energy in good writing.

Writing experiences for teachers

✔ Look back over some of your previous writer's notebook entries. Underline the verbs. Then see if you can find several that could be improved. Cross out the weaker verb and write the stronger verb into your piece.

✔ Do several other pieces, and then go back and re-read, paying special attention to verbs, looking for even one or two verb choices that could be changed to make the piece stronger. For example: Write about your most memorable day—either good or bad—as a teacher. Write about something—or someone—who really makes you angry. Tell why. Tell how this situation or person makes you feel. Write about what you would do if you were made principal for the week. If you're already a principal, write about what you would do if you were the district superintendent.

Classroom experiences for young writers

As you become more conscious of verb choice and the power verbs have to help writers create a vivid picture for readers, you'll find yourself looking for ways to share this power with your students. Of course, you will model verb choice as you talk in the classroom. They will begin to use the verbs that they routinely hear you use. As those verbs become part of the spoken vocabulary in your classroom, you will notice that students try them out in their writing.

But that's not enough. You have to model the use of strong verbs in your own writing in the classroom. Whether you are modeling the first draft of a piece or working to revise a piece with students, think out loud about selecting just the right verb to create the desired image in your readers' minds.

Teachers at Clark Elementary School know that they want their students to be precise in their word choice, that they want their young writers to use strong, active verbs that convey exact meaning. So the Clark teachers use those types of verbs in classroom conversation with students. And they model the use of these verbs as they write with their classes:

> "Saturday I came home from the grocery store," Priscilla Towner tells her fourth graders. " I wasn't wearing my glasses, so I couldn't see clearly, but I noticed there was something dark on the floor. As I dumped an armful of bags on the counter, I thought to myself that one of the boys had left a piece of rope there. As I reached over to put the milk in the refrigerator, the 'rope' slithered under the 'fridge.
>
> "Snake! I screamed. In my panic, I dropped the remaining bag and oranges scattered everywhere. As I bent down to begin picking them up, that snake slithered from underneath the 'fridge and stopped right by the orange I was reaching for."

Priscilla's students listen with rapt attention as she finishes telling her story. Their comments and questions let her know that her story, with its strong verbs, created a vivid image for her students.

After a brief discussion, she moves into her writing craft lesson. On this particular day, she has chosen to show her students how to develop an event in a story. As she models writing about a story event for her students, Priscilla makes sure that she thinks aloud about her verb choice decisions. She has taught her fourth graders to listen for strong verbs, to look for them as they read, and to use them when they write. And now, these young writers are able to make verb choices that bring their writing to life.

A few miles away at Temple Terrace Elementary School, Kelli Hicks works on verb choices with first and second grade writers. Kelli typically begins her writing workshop with a piece of literature that allows her children to hear a polished example of what she wants them to do. Today, she reads aloud *The Wind Blew* and then writes the action words on a chart as students remember and name them.

Kelli distributes pictures of animals and asks her students to think of action words that would match their animal. While the students are thinking, she displays a story about a trip to the zoo for the class to revise. Today the focus is on revising to use verbs that describe what the animals do. As the class revises the story, the child with the animal picture that matches the animal in the story gives a more precise verb to replace the one in the story. Following the revision, the story is read aloud and students discuss how their verb choices made their piece better.

The young writers are now ready to apply what they just learned. They pull their writing folders out of their desks and begin writing. Some students return to pieces in progress to look for weak verbs to be replaced with stronger ones. Others begin writing new pieces, mindful of verb choice as they write. But whether they are revising or writing a new piece, the students are focusing on selecting verbs that match what the character in their story is doing.

Finally, the writers are ready to share. As they read their stories aloud, classmates comment on the verbs used and Kelli adds them to the growing list on the class chart. She smiles, knowing that her writers will return to the chart again and again as they become more conscious of the power of verbs, and verb choice becomes more precise and powerful in their writing.

References

Lesser, C. (1997) *Storm in the desert.* San Diego: Harcourt Brace.
Martin, B. (1993) *Old devil wind.* San Diego: Harcourt Brace.

Crafting Engaging Leads: The Beginnings for Good Writing

6

Some books grab you in the very first sentence. They're like quicksand—they suck you in, sentence by sentence, from the very first. These writers have mastered the art of effective lead-writing.

- Like Lois Lowry in *The Giver:*

    It was almost December, and Jonas was beginning to be frightened.

- Or Steven Kellogg, in *Best Friends:*

    Louise Jenkins and I love horses, but we aren't allowed to have real ones.

- Or Jane Yolen in *Owl Moon:*

    It was late one winter night, long past my bedtime, when Pa and I went owling.

- Or Jerry Spinelli in *Maniac Magee:*

    They say Maniac Magee was born in a dump. They say his stomach was a cereal box and his heart a sofa spring.

Good leads aren't necessarily easy to write. In fact, many professional writers spend longer on the first few sentences of their books than they do on any other element. As you read some of their secrets—and try some of the techniques we suggest in this chapter—you'll watch your own leads improve and get new ideas for teaching students how to craft attention-grabbing beginning sentences.

Types of Leads

There's no one right way to write a lead. You might begin by describing a scene where a story is to take place. Or maybe by describing an important character. Beginning with dialogue can often pull a reader into a story. And some writers love to start right on top of the action (the conflict or problem in the story) so that the reader is involved from the very first sentence.

Look at these options for leads:

- ***Begin with the problem:*** Narratives are chronological re-tellings of events; stories have a conflict or problem. And some writers enjoy crafting leads that immediately put the reader right in the middle of the action. That's the way John Reynolds Gardiner began his classic novel *Stone Fox:*

    > One day grandfather wouldn't get out of bed. He just lay there and stared at the ceiling and looked sad. (p. 3)

- ***Begin with description:*** Sometimes writers want to paint a verbal picture so that readers can picture the setting of the story, as Tony Johnston (1994) did in *Amber on the Mountain:*

    > Amber lived on a mountain so high, it poked through the clouds like a needle stuck in down. Trees bristled on it like porcupine quills. And the air made you giddy—it was that clear. Still, for all that soaring beauty, Amber was lonesome. For mountain people lived scattered far from one another. (p. 5)

- ***Begin with dialogue:*** Stories that begin with dialogue give readers the impression that they have entered the scene in the middle of a conversation. They want to know more. Mark Twain (1876/1946) began one of America's most famous novels, *The Adventures of Tom Sawyer,* with dialogue:

    > "Tom?"
    > No answer.
    > "Tom!"
    > No answer.
    > "What's gone with that boy, I wonder? You Tom!" (p. 1)

- ***Begin with an introduction:*** Occasionally writers will begin stories by introducing themselves. Charles Dickens (1861/1996) let Pip introduce himself in the opening lines of Great Expectations:

    > My father's family name being Pirrip, and my Christian name Philip, my infant tongue could make of both names nothing longer or more explicit than Pip. So I called myself Pip, and came to be called Pip. (p. 23)

- ***Begin by introducing a character with a pronoun, but withhold the name:*** Some writers introduce a main character in the lead, but do not identify that character until they have described him or her or told a story about that character. That's how Ernest Hemingway (1952) began *The Old Man and the Sea:*

    > He was an old man who fished alone in a skiff in the Gulf Stream and he had gone eighty-four days now without taking a fish. In the first forty days a boy had been with him. (p. 9)

Obviously, there's no one right way to begin a story or a poem. And though leads might describe a character or setting, or drop the reader into the middle of a conversation, or immediately present a dilemma we want to know more about, they have one thing in common: These points of entry were chosen by the writer to involve the reader in a key element of the story. The writer had to ask such questions as:

✔ What is this story or piece of expository writing *about*?

✔ What will readers be most interested in?

✔ What techniques (dialogue, description, plot) could I share with readers that would involve them immediately in the story and make them want to read more?

How does any writer—child or adult—learn to write better leads? The answers are deceptively simple:

- **Pay attention to leads:** In other words, read like a writer. When you read a lead and like it, look at what the writer did. Ask yourself how you might be able to use that technique yourself. Also, the lead styles the writers have identified in this chapter are not exhaustive. These are popular types of leads, but there are many more. In your writer's notebook, list these lead types and add to them. As you read books whose leads illustrate various lead approaches, expand your list.

- **Take leads seriously:** Most professional writers spend more time on leads than anything else. As your writing improves, you'll probably note that you spend a disproportionate time on the first few paragraphs of any piece. But that doesn't mean you just work on leads until you get them right. Go ahead and write, trying to get anything down that will help you keep on writing. But then go back and spend time with the lead improving it, re-writing it, trying different approaches.

- **Try different approaches:** We tend to fall into writing ruts, continuing to use the lead formulas with which we're most comfortable. Perhaps you really enjoy writing descriptive leads. After you finish a piece, try another approach with the lead and compare it with your descriptive. Deliberately step outside your writing box.

Writing experiences for teachers

✔ What's your favorite lead in either children's or adult literature? Why does it work? How might you adapt it to something you write someday? Find that lead you especially like and copy it into your writer's notebook. Then analyze it and tell why it works.

✔ Go back and re-visit some of the pieces you've written since you began working through *Absolutely Write!*. Try different lead approaches. Don't rewrite everything—just the lead and maybe the next few paragraphs after it, just enough to try a different approach to your pieces. Try some of the approaches outlined in this chapter.

Classroom experiences for young writers

Some professional writers agonize over their leads. Famed *New York Times* sports-writer Red Smith said he wrote by sitting at a typewriter and "opening a vein." So if good leads can be difficult for professionals, how do you teach second graders, fifth graders—any of your students—to write them?

The answer? Use the resources at hand.

Classrooms and media centers are filled with these books and magazines, the resources for teaching leads. We turn to those very writers who craft the leads that pull us right into what they have written. We find their books and articles and use them to show our students what effective leads look like. We also model for our students how we write leads, and sometimes, when we have written boring leads, we show them how to revise to begin the piece with a more engaging lead.

In short, we flood our classrooms with models of engaging leads.

Laura Burek knows this, so she pays special attention to leads as she reads. She has the media specialist look out for books and magazine articles that have effective leads. She exchanges selections with her teaching partner. These resources become models in her writing workshop craft lessons to focus on different types of leads. She shows her fourth graders how to vary leads to grab their readers' attention and to fit the type of writing they are doing.

Taking advantage of her fourth graders' flair for the dramatic, she uses Carol Sonenklar's (2000) *Bug Girl* to show her writers a lead with a dramatic twist:

> There I was, crouched in a dark corner. I was invisible; perfectly camouflaged in the leaves and branches. My deadly assault was feared far and wide. Nothing could get by me.
>
> And then I spotted something. Something desirable. Something delicious. It had no idea that just a few inches away, a hunter was lurking. My forceful arms and legs, alive with sensory vibrations, were itching to move. When I was ready to trap it in my death grip, I could bound at superspeed.
>
> I was, a killer.
> Meet Charlie Kaplan, Assassin.
> Assassin bug, that it. (pg. 3)

How could you put this book down? Who is Charlie Kaplan? What's going on here? You have to read more; you have to find out. This lead pulls readers, especially young readers, right into the story.

Laura shows her students other techniques for introducing characters in a narrative lead. They write stories where the main character is introduced in the lead. They model their own leads after others they enjoy. Kate DiCamillo's (2000) Because of Winn Dixie shows them how to use a character and an ordinary act to make the reader want more:

> My name is India Opal Buloni, and last summer my daddy, the preacher, sent me to the store for a box of macaroni and cheese, some white rice, and two tomatoes and I came back with a dog.

> This is what happened: I walked into the produce section of the Winn-Dixie grocery store to pick out my two tomatoes and I almost bumped right into the store manager. He was standing there all red- faced, screaming and waving his arms around.
>
> "Who let a dog in here?" he kept on shouting. "Who let a dirty dog in here?" (pg. 7)

Laura encourages her students to use sensory details in descriptive leads and uses Alice Dalgliesh's (1954) Newbery Honor book, *The Courage of Sarah Noble* to show them how:

> Sarah lay on a quilt under a tree. The darkness was all around her, but through the branches she could see one bright star. It was comfortable to look at.
>
> The spring night was cold, and Sarah drew her warm cloak close. That was comfortable, too. She thought of how her mother had put it around her the day she and her father started out on this long, hard journey. (p. 1)

They learn to introduce a character with a brief description the same way William Steig (1993) did in *Shrek!*

> His mother was ugly and his father was ugly, but Shrek was uglier than the two of them put together. By the time he toddled, Shrek could spit flame a full nine yards and vent smoke from either ear. With just a look he cowed the reptiles in the swamp. Any snake dumb enough to bite him instantly got convulsions and died. (p. 1)

Laura continues to use literature to show her students other kinds of leads. They learn to lead with:

✔ background information
✔ dialogue
✔ a problem
✔ flashbacks
✔ a startling fact

She teaches them to use literary devices selectively in their leads as well as in the body of their pieces:

- You can hear the explosion of repetitive consonant sounds as they use *alliteration* to get their readers' attention.

  "Good grief," growled Greg as he stared at the disaster in his room.

- Other pieces begin with words that imitate the sounds associated with an action. Evidence that they have learned to get a reader's attention with *onomatopoeia*.

  KA-BOOM! Mr. Oliver stared at the class as his face turned from its usual tan to red and then to purple.

- The young writers create pictures for readers by leading with *similes:*

    It was my first day in my new school and I was nervous until the principal introduced me to my teacher. He was as big as an elephant. Nervous quickly became terror.

  - Or they use *hyperbole:*

    "I've told you a million times not to climb out that window," my mom yelled at me as I dangled by my jacket from a limb outside my bedroom window.

Laura's students want to know how to use many kinds of leads. They collect their favorite leads, copy and post them prominently in the classroom. This display becomes a resource for writers when they are stuck and need help.

They collect interesting or unusual headlines from newspapers and write articles to match the headlines. Then they compare their leads and articles with the original.

Sometimes, Laura provides a collection of books and asks the students to read only the leads, looking for examples of the type of lead they have been working on. This allows them to see how different authors use the same technique.

Laura's students also return to pieces in their writing folders to look for mundane beginnings that they turn into inviting leads. These writers know that sometimes the right lead may not come when they first begin a piece, but they write the piece anyway, knowing they will have the opportunity to revise, if needed. Assessment of their own writing, and decisions about revision are routine in this classroom.

The young writers in Laura's classroom know the value of an engaging lead. They want their writing to be read, so they read and pay attention to the leads. They study and practice the craft of writing engaging leads. And every time they write another lead that grabs their readers' attention, they demonstrate their growth as writers.

References

Dalgliesh, A. (1954). *The courage of Sarah Noble.* New York: Macmillan Publishing.

Dickens, C. (1996). *Great expectations.* Boston and New York: Bedford Books.

DiCamillo, K. (2000). *Because of Winn Dixie.* Cambridge, Mass.: Candlewick Press.

Gardiner, J. (1980). *Stone fox.* New York: Harper Trophy.

Hemingway, E. (1952). *The old man and the sea.* New York: Charles Scribner's Sons.

Johnston, T. (1994). *Amber on the mountain.* New York: Dial.

Sonenklar, C. (2000). *Bug girl.* New York: Dell Yearling.

Steig, W. (1993). *Shrek!* New York: Farrar, Straus and Giroux.

Twain, M. (Clemens, S.). (1946). *The adventures of Tom Sawyer.* Cleveland and New York: The World Pub. Co.

Writing Dialogue:
Putting Readers into the Story

7

Good dialogue makes stories sound real and brings characters to life. We can *tell* what characters did. Better yet, we can *show* readers what they did by writing visually and painting pictures in readers' minds. But when we take good storytelling and insert dialogue, we put readers inside the story. They can overhear characters speak as the story unfolds before them.

Writing teacher Clive Matson (1998) tells his workshops about the power of good dialogue:

> Dialogue confers zest and the 'wildness of life' to writing. There is dialogue when any character speaks and when that happens, the written word seems to stand up, open its mouth, and start talking. Dialogue shows what is happening at the moment—out loud.
>
> Dialogue displays what is consuming the character. Is the character angry? Bewildered? Happy? That feeling vibrates through the words when we imagine them spoken.
>
> The thoughts behind that feeling and the issues engaging the character give the dialogue its flavor. The character seems to come alive. (p. 105).

Why Writers Use Dialogue

Effective use of dialogue by a writer begins with that writer's understanding of what dialogue is and what it does. It's not just filling space between chunks of narrative. When you were in school, your teachers might have made the same type of mistake with dialogue that we mentioned discussing descriptive writing in Workshop 4. A teacher who told you just to add details without telling you why might also have told you to add dialogue because you didn't have any.

That's *not* the reason writers use dialogue. A writer wouldn't think "I haven't inserted any dialogue in two pages, so I'd better put some in." Writers use dialogue to make their characters sound real, to reveal character, and to tell the story itself. Re-read Bill Martin Jr.'s (1985) *Ghost-Eye Tree* as a study in writing dialogue. Much of the story line itself is revealed in conversations between the two main characters.

So does dialogue make a story involving or fun to read? Not all dialogue. For instance, what's duller than a court transcript, and it's pure dialogue between lawyers, witnesses, and a judge. But in the hands of a crime novelist—one who takes that dialogue, edits it, and shapes what the character says to make it artful and revealing—dialogue can give you a can't-put-it-down story.

How do you learn to write good dialogue? Several techniques have proved helpful for many writers:

- **Listen:** Your world is crowded with voices. Every day, you hear adults and children complaining, explaining, directing, greeting, telling stories, lying. What you're hearing is the stuff of dialogue—if you listen to the rhythms of the speech around you. It may be helpful to carry a palm-sized microcassette player for a few days. Just put it in your shirt pocket or purse or on your desk. Record conversations in the check-out line or on the playground. It'll show you how people actually talk. You'll find that listening, really listening, isn't easy because we train ourselves to tune out language. Writers have to get into the habit of tuning in again. Writer Tom Chiarella (1998) calls it *crowding*. By that, he means getting in close enough to conversations that you can listen unobtrusively. He explains:

    How do you do it? Take one step closer. Lean in slightly. Make yourself as quiet as you can and stare straight ahead. It's important to remember that when I use the term "crowding," I do not mean physical crowding. I mean conscious listening. I mean stealing the words from the air around you. It's a different relationship to the world. It is, I believe, one facet of the writer's relationship to the world. You are tuning in. (p. 14)

    Your mother probably called it eavesdropping. She was right, but it's one of those forgivable sins for writers. We have to listen if we want to learn to write good dialogue.

- **Write snippets of dialogue:** You might begin by transcribing, say, a conversation at your desk with a child who came up to tell you her stomach ached and ask for permission to go to the nurse's office. Or a colleague's complaints about her meddling mother-in-law. Or a friend's explanation of why she will miss your Christmas party. Write these short dialogues as if they appeared in stories you were writing. Forget context. You don't need introductions or conclusions. Putting speech tags (he said) is optional. You may just record the conversation or a part of it on paper, starting a new paragraph every time the speaker changes.

- *Balance dialogue with other techniques of good writing:* In your own reading, look for ways writers employ dialogue. You'll notice that the books you enjoy typically do not have long stretches of uninterrupted dialogue. Look at what else you find:

  ✔ Interior monologue: Writers tell what characters are thinking, in addition to what they are saying in dialogue.

  ✔ Description that helps readers picture the scene: Writers help readers picture the scene and the people in which the characters are talking.

  ✔ Narrative: Writers tell stories, using dialogue aspects of the characters and their personalities that simple narrative never could.

- *Pay attention to skillful uses of dialogue in your reading:* One of the best ways to learn to write dialogue is to get a "feel" for its use in the books you enjoy. Most readers, like most moviegoers, never notice the techniques of writing and cinema. But perhaps you took a film genre course in college that introduced you to cinematography and now you notice camera angles, lighting and film editing. This doesn't detract from your enjoyment of the movie—rather, it adds to it because you can enjoy the movie both for its technical aspects and its narrative line. You can do the same thing with books as you pay attention to dialogue: everything from how it is punctuated, to how it fits into the story, to how it interplays with interior monologue, to how a writer chooses whether to quote directly or summarize.

As you begin to write dialogue, to teach craft lessons in dialogue, and to coach your young writers in effective dialogue, you will come to appreciate more and more how the writers you enjoy use dialogue effectively. As you learn from your own reading, you'll be able to take those lessons back to the classroom.

Writing experiences for teachers

One of the best ways to practice dialogue is to turn newspaper cartoons into scenes for your writer's notebook. It's simple. Find a favorite cartoon in Sunday's newspaper (Sunday cartoons have more panels and thus allow for more practice). Choose something that tells a complete story from begin to end that day, rather than a cartoon with a continuing story line left over from previous weeks. When you look, say, at *Peanuts* or *Garfield,* what do you see? A complete story told only in dialogue and interior monologue. So take that story and tell it yourself, as a narrative, in your writer's notebook. You'll have to add, with words, the information the artist shows visually. Let's say the first scene shows Snoopy lying on top of his doghouse wearing his World War I fighter ace garb. He's thinking about facing the Red Baron. You might begin your story like this:

> Lying atop his doghouse, Snoopy gazed into the late afternoon sky, his pilot's goggles perched on his head and his scarf hanging from his neck.

His thoughts drifted to his air nemesis, the Red Baron.
"Just wait until tomorrow morning," Snoopy addressed his ab-
sent foe, "when I will earn my final victory over you, Red Baron."

Get the idea? Turning cartoons into stories allows you to work with dialogue while developing your ability to set a scene and describe for your reader. Remember, you must do the same thing with your words that the cartoonist does with pictures.

✔ Review the basics of punctuating dialogue. If you master these rules, you'll have pretty much everything you need to write dialogue successfully.

- Periods and commas go inside quotes, all the time. These examples are correct:

    "Just wait until tomorrow morning," Snoopy said.
    Snoopy called out to his foe, "You don't have a chance."

- If the quote asks a question or forms an exclamation, those marks go inside the quotation marks also. These examples are correct:

    "Are you ready for battle?" Snoopy asked.
    "Curse you, Red Baron!" Snoopy shouted.

- Commas or periods never follow question marks or exclamation points. Look at the two sentences just preceding. You'd never put a comma after the question mark following the word *battle* or the exclamation point following *Baron*.

- When the speech tag comes in the middle of a sentence of dialogue, it acts as a pause, set off by commas and surrounded on either side by parts of the quotation. The following is correct:

    "Tomorrow we will fight again," Snoopy said, "and this time I will be victorious."

- If two people speak without pause, or without a speech tag between them, you begin a new paragraph each time a new speaker says something. Don't worry about one-sentence paragraphs, or even one-word paragraphs. They are correct in this case, because you are using paragraphing to denote a change in speaker. Note this example of dialogue in J. K. Rowling's (1998) *Harry Potter and the Sorcerer's Stone*. Harry and his friends were caught out of bed late one night at the Hogwarts School, and Professor McGonagall tells them that they will be assessed detentions and 50 points will be deducted from their residence house, Gryffindor. See how Rowling handles the dialogue:

    "Fifty?" Harry gasped—they would lose the lead, the lead he'd won in the last Quiddich match.
    "Fifty points *each*," said Professor McGonagall, breathing heavily through her long, pointed nose.
    "Professor—please—"
    "You *can't*—"

"Don't tell me what I can and can't do, Potter. Now get
back to bed, all of you. I've never been more ashamed of
Gryffindor students."

A hundred and fifty points lost.... Harry felt as though
the bottom had dropped out of his stomach. (p. 244)

Note the exchange between Harry and Professor McGonagall. At first, Rowling uses speech tags (*Harry gasped* and *said Professor McGonagall*) to establish the identities of the speakers. Then she drops the speech tags altogether, beginning a new paragraph with each new statement to mark the change in speakers. Finally, note how Rowling switches back to narrative in the last paragraph to continue the story.

One more thing: Some teachers are near-obsessed with providing variety in speech tags. If you say *said* in one paragraph, you should follow it with explained and stated and barked and whined and bellowed and shouted and protested and cooed and coaxed and coughed and chortled and stuttered and stammered, ad nauseum.

But think. When's the last time you heard someone chortle a statement, or cough, or bark one? The most frequent speech tag used by professional writers is just plain old *said.* It is used far more than all other speech tags combined. When's the last time you heard someone who just finished a novel say, "You gotta read this book! The speech tags are wonderful!" The function of a speech tag is just to tell the reader who said something; the dialogue itself is what should be engaging.

Pick up a favorite paperback, one you don't mind marking in. Scan a chapter and highlight several pages of quotes. Go back and see what speech tags are used and how the quotes were punctuated. It's a great review of how writers actually use the mechanics of dialogue.

✔ Go to a public place to eavesdrop on dialogue. A fast-food restaurant, an athletic event, an airport all make great locations. Listen in using the crowding technique discussed earlier in this chapter, then write what you heard. Just take notes on several exchanges. Write quickly and move on to another conversation. Take quick notes on the participants, like: "argument between teen-ager with a Mohawk and a ring in his ear and his father, wearing expensive-looking three-piece suit." Then, write down as much as you can. When you get home, go back and reproduce one of the conversations in your writer's notebook, using speech tags and brief descriptions of the participants in the conversation. Reproducing a real-life conversation can help you get the flavor of actual speech.

✔ Try your own hand at dialogue. To make it easier, set up a scene in which two people are arguing (that gives you a real back-and-forth that makes for easier dialogue). You choose the topic—maybe a husband and wife arguing over money, or two children arguing over whatever's most typical for students in your class to argue about. Set a scene, briefly describe the characters, then use dialogue and even interior monologue (to show what the characters are thinking while they are talking).

Classroom experiences for young writers

Chad is eager to share his story in a conference with his teacher, Felicia Brown.

"Why don't you read the part you like best?" she asks the eager fourth-grader. So Chad begins to read his experiment with using dialogue:

> "Hi, Joey," I said.
> "Hi, yourself," Joey said to me.
> "What are you doing?" I asked.
> "Nothing. What are you doing?" said Joey.
> "Nothing," I said back.
> "Do you want to play with me?" Joey asked.

Felicia talked with Chad for a few minutes about his story, but she made a mental note that his problem was common to many of her students—boring, meaningless dialogue. Dialogue that fails to move the story along and, in fact, slows it to a crawl; dialogue that doesn't give any insight into the characters, doesn't help us to know what they are thinking or what their relationship is; dialogue that makes no contribution to the story.

This type of dialogue was typical of Felicia's students' writing at the beginning of the year. Not only were her third graders writing like this, but the fourth graders in this new multi-age class weren't doing much better. The fourth grade writers could punctuate the dialogue, but it had no life, made no contribution to their stories. So Felicia began her plans to replace boring and meaningless with lively, purposeful dialogue.

She decided to begin with Beverly Cleary's (1979) *Ramona and Her Mother.* Her students were familiar with it. In fact, it was one of their favorites. For her mini-lesson, she selected a conversation that took place at dinner following an argument between Ramona's parents.

> She felt all churned up inside, as if she didn't know whether to cry or to burst out of the house shouting, "My mother and father had a fight!"
> "Please pass the butter." Mrs. Quimby might have been speaking to a stranger.
> "May I please have the syrup?" Mr. Quimby asked politely.
> "The funniest thing happened at school," said Beezus, and Ramona understood that her sister was anxious to start a conversation that would smooth things over and make their parents forget their quarrel, perhaps make them laugh.
> After a moment of silence Mrs. Quimby said, "Tell me."
> "You'll never guess how a boy spelled relief in a spelling test," said Beezus.
> "How?" asked Ramona to help the conversation along. Mr. Quimby silently served himself two more hot cakes.
> "He spelled it r-o-l-a-i-d-s," said Beezus, looking anxiously at her parents, who actually smiled.

> Ramona did not smile. "But the man on television spells relief that way. He said r-o-l-a-i-d-s spells relief. I've heard him."
> "Silly," said Beezus, but this time she spoke with affection. That's just a slogan. Relief is r-e-l-i-e-f." (p. 105)

Through careful questions Felicia guided her students to see how the dialogue shows readers that Mr. and Mrs. Quimby are still angry with each other and how Beezus and Ramona feel about the situation. Beverly Cleary's dialogue gives insight into how the characters are feeling. She also uses Beezus' contribution to the conversation to show how she is trying to alleviate the situation. It is easy to see here that the parents are cool to each other because they are still angry, and that Beezus and Ramona are apprehensive and want their parents to be happy with each other—and with the kids.

Knowing that her students need to see how this type of meaningful dialogue is written and to hear an author's thinking as they write it, Felicia moves to the overhead projector. She begins to write about an argument that she had with her 5-year old daughter about what to wear to school, including dialogue that allows her students to visualize the scene in the Brown household that morning. As she writes, she thinks out loud so the students can see the decisions she makes as a writer.

Following Felicia's modeled writing, the students write about an argument that they might have with a sibling or friend. Felicia moves about the room conferencing with students as they write, focusing her comments and questions on the dialogues they are writing.

Felicia's writers need lots of models and practice to become fluent in writing dialogue that moves the story along, that gives the reader a mental image of the characters. Over the next few weeks she provides this practice in a variety of ways:

✔ Students look for and collect examples of effective dialogue in the books they read. These are displayed and referred to. They discuss how the dialogue moves the story along or tells more about a character.

✔ They return to pieces in their writing folders to look for and replace statements with dialogue. Statements like *My dad told me to do my homework* are replaced with, "It's time you got busy on that math homework," Dad said as he looked at the clock for the third time.

✔ Felicia gives students cards that have a character and a personality trait (example: an eager baseball player). They write one line of dialogue that gives the reader insight into the character (example: "I can't wait until it's my turn to bat. I'm going to slam a home run over the fence!" the Red Sox catcher shouted to the coach.)

✔ Other books are used as models for the writing dialogue:

  • Steven Kellogg's (1997) retelling of *The Three Little Pigs* is used to show how to use dialogue for giving insight into a character's personality or to build up to action in the story.

- The classic *Charlotte's Web,* by E. B. White (1952), becomes the book that children reach for and pore over to find examples of various kinds of dialogue.

- Caldecott Honor Book *Mufaro's Beautiful Daughters* by John Steptoe (1987), is used to demonstrate dialogue that moves the story along.

As the weeks pass Felicia's third- and fourth-grade writers learn to use dialogue more purposefully and effectively. The typical dialogue seen at the beginning of the year has been replaced with:

> I looked up from counting the cracks in the sidewalk on the way to school and saw the class bully blocking my way.
> "Hi, Joey," I said.
> There was no answer. Joey just stood there, blocking my way.
> "What are you doing?" I asked.
> "Guarding my part of the sidewalk," he answered.
> I knew that I would be late for school again.

References

Chiarella, T. (1998). *Writing dialogue.* Cincinnati: Story Press.

Cleary, B. (1979). *Ramona and her mother.* New York: Avon Books.

Kellogg, S. (1997). *The three little pigs.* New York: William Morrow and Co.

Martin, B. (1985). *The ghost-eye tree.* New York: Henry Holt.

Matson, C. (1998). *Let the crazy child write!* Novato, Calif.: New World Library.

Rowling, J. K. (1998). *Harry Potter and the sorcerer's stone.* New York: Scholastic.

Steptoe, J. (1987). *Mufaro's beautiful daughters.* New York: Scholastic.

White, E. (1952). *Charlotte's web.* New York: Harper and Row.

Read Like a Writer:
Learning to Write from the Authors You Love

Kids who love sports understand this principle instinctively.

On Sunday afternoons, they watch their favorite NFL teams on television. But as soon as the game is over, or maybe even during halftime, you can find them in the yard or the street or the playground, playing football. And as they play, they imitate what they have just seen on TV. Perhaps they were introduced to the flea-flicker—a play where the quarterback hands off to a running back, who suddenly turns and tosses the ball back to the quarterback. Because the defense saw a running play developing, defenders are now looking to tackle a running back. That means receivers are more likely open for a pass. The quarterback takes the tossback from his running back and throws it to an open receiver.

It's a trick play that isn't used very much, so kids might not know the name or the technique. But if they see a flea-flicker completed for a long gain, you can bet that's the play they want to try in their schoolyard games. Nobody told them this was a play they should try. The announcers did not explain it in detail or give them a worksheet to reinforce the basic principles of the flea-flicker. They were not urged to try it on their own. They just saw something that worked and couldn't wait to give it a try. When kids watch football, they watch to enjoy the game. But always—in the back of their minds—is the idea that what these NFL guys are doing, they can do too.

Writers approach their reading in the same way. They read to enjoy, but always—in the back of their minds—they are looking for techniques and methods and concepts; anything they can try themselves in their writing. Novelist William Faulkner put it this way in his advice to young writers:

> Read, read, read. Read everything—trash, classics, good and
> bad, and see how they do it. Just like a carpenter who works as
> an apprentice and studies the master. Read! You'll absorb it. Then
> write. If it is good, you'll find out. If it's not, throw it out the window.

What are You Looking for When You Read?

When you begin to read like a writer—to see the books and periodicals you read as source materials for your own writing and your writing instruction—you'll never again lack a topic for your craft lessons, an illustration for some point you are teaching young writers, or the inspiration to try new things in your own writing.

So what are some of the characteristics of good writing you can find in your reading, imitate in your writing, and teach in your classes? Let's take just two characteristics of good writing, to see how we can pull these from our reading:

> ***Bring abstract ideas to life:*** Good writers don't talk about poverty and injustice and evil, or even kindness or generosity. Those are abstractions. Effective writing turns those abstract concepts into concrete reality. Poet Brod Bagert has written poems which take abstract character qualities and embody them in concrete characters kids can relate to. And what's more abstract than the concept of *goodness?* In our 21st century world, what does it mean to be *good?* Bagert (1997) has embodied that abstraction in a real poetic example. Read and enjoy, but at the same time, note how the poet uses real-life stories and description to bring life to the abstraction:

Mirror Image

Brod Bagert

> I could hardly believe it.
> Everywhere I looked,
> People were being nice to each other.
>
>> Like Mr. Washington.
>> He takes a walk every morning,
>> And when he passes the house where an old person lives,
>> He picks up the newspapers
>> And throws it closer to the door.
>>
>> And Philip's big sister?
>> She visits her grandmother every day
>> And reads to her.
>>
>> And when Mrs. Francis feeds the birds.
>> Every evening like clockwork,
>> Just before the sun goes down,
>> She's out there feeding birds.
>
> Everywhere I looked,
> I saw good in other people,
> And I thought they were all changing.

> But now I understand,
> They haven't changed at all.
> It's my eyes that are changing,
> These earth-anointed eyes
> That somehow now can see
> The good in other people
> As the goodness grows in me.

It's one thing to talk about goodness, but quite another to tell about Mr. Washington picking up papers and Philip's big sister reading to her grandmother and Mrs. Francis feeding the birds. Good writing has a lot of visual images and strong active verbs and concrete nouns. Look at these paragraphs telling about Nedry's encounter with a dinosaur in Michael Crichton's (1990) *Jurassic Park:*

> Nedry opened the car door, glancing back at the dinosaur to make sure it wasn't going to attack, and felt a sudden excruciating pain in his eyes, stabbing like spikes into the back of his skull, and he squeezed his eyes shut and gasped with the intensity of it and threw up his hands to cover his eyes and felt the slippery foam trickling down both sides of his nose. Spit. The dinosaur had spit in his eyes.
> Even as he realized it, the pain overwhelmed him, and he dropped to his knees, disoriented, wheezing. He collapsed onto his side, his cheek pressed to the wet ground, his breath coming in thin whistles through the constant, ever-screaming pain that caused flashing spots of light to appear behind his tightly shut eyelids. (p. 96).

As we find passages like that in our reading, we look again to notice its strength— concrete detail painted in word pictures.

Varying sentence structure. Good writers offer different types of sentence structures and differing lengths and sentences. *Really* good writers allow the structure of the sentence to reflect what's going on in the text. Longer sentences and more clauses slow down the pace of a sentence. Shorter sentences speed it up. Anne Bernays and Pamela Painter (1991) share a way writers can check their sentence structure for readability:

> John Updike says that the best way to get the kinks out of your prose is to read it aloud. Reading aloud what you have written reveals its flaws in the same way a magnifying glass reveals blemishes on your skin.
> Keep in mind that the eye and ear are connected and that what the reader sees will somehow be transmitted to his inner ear. Too many sentences with a similar construction will make your reader yawn. You should always read your work aloud before showing it to anyone. Doing this will help you avoid monotony, repetition, flatness, unintentional alliteration, and other impediments to smooth, fluid prose. (p. 186).

Notice how Lois Lowry (1993) uses this concept in the very first paragraph of her Newbery classic *The Giver.* She begins by telling the reader that Jonas was "beginning to be frightened." The second sentence stands in sharp contrast and contradiction: just the one word, "no." Her sentences get longer as she begins to explain. Note also the variety of grammatical structures in her sentences. Her opening sentences are shorter, with a basic subject/verb/object order. Then she brings in a longer sentence, beginning with an introductory participle phrase ("squinting toward the sky"). She ends the paragraph with another more complex sentence which actually has the subject as the last word in the sentence (plane) and an unstated verb.

> It was almost December, and Jonas was beginning to be frightened. No. Wrong word, Jonas thought. Frightened meant that deep, sickening feeling of something terrible about to happen. Frightened was the way he had felt a year ago when an unidentified aircraft had overflown the community twice. He had seen it both times. Squinting toward the sky, he had seen the sleek jet, almost a blur at its high speed, go past, and a second later heard the blast of sound that followed. Then one more time, a moment later, from the opposite direction, the same plane. (p. 1).

Was Lois Lowry consciously thinking of sentence variety when she wrote that paragraph? Most surely not. Is it something you can work on as you write? Again, probably not. But that's the value of reading like a writer. You begin to notice sentence variety because you're looking for it. And sometimes you find a passage you especially like in a book and you are totally caught up in the story—reading like a reader, not a writer. But because you found it so engaging, you go back and re-read several pages, this time as a writer. And you begin to look for the techniques the writer used to reel you in. Perhaps one of those is sentence variety; you would never have found it if you hadn't been looking. And because you become sensitive to it over a period of time, you actually begin to look at sentence variety in what you write. Then you find yourself writing about a race you ran in as a teen-ager. You led the pack, along with one more competitor, the two of you running neck and neck as you sprinted toward the finish line. As you write about your final sprint, your sentences become longer, almost breathless in pace, reflecting the race itself. And then, as you cross the finish line, the race over, your sentences get shorter, perhaps something like: Victory! I couldn't believe it! I had won. I really had won.

Facility with using sentence variety comes with fluency in writing and paying attention to how professional stylists use the technique. Before we move on, let's recapitulate the concept; the explanation is David Carroll's (1995) in his writer-friendly book *A Manual of Writer's Tricks:*

> Writers are weavers, and sentences are their threads. After several long sentences use a short one. After several short ones, a long one. Then a medium. Then two shorties. Keep varying the

length and rhythm of word combinations. Throw in a single word now and then. Or a short question. After it place a winding, several-claused sentence as a counterpoint.

Ditto for paragraphs. Too many long paragraphs appear forbidding. Too many short ones seem superficial. If your paragraphs all tend to run approximately the same lengths, your readers will become bored. Keep varying things.

It's not that people consciously notice sentence or paragraph lengths. It's subliminal, but nonetheless very real. Such elements are among the so-called "indefinables" that are responsible for the production of good writing, and bad. (p. 54–55).

Sentence variety is difficult to teach. The key is being aware of the technique when you find it in a piece you enjoy. As you become aware of sentence variety, and make your students aware, you find your own pieces and those of your students showing more variety in sentence structure and length.

· · · · · · ·

These were only two examples of how writers use their reading to develop their writing. But good writing teachers build their writing curriculum on such examples, as they take books students enjoy and look at the technique behind them. Filmmakers do this all the time. After every major special-effects-oriented motion picture, someone does a documentary on how the movie was made. At first, we sit through the latest *Star Wars* epic, engrossed in the story. But then we watch the documentary to see how George Lucas put the magic on the screen. We see computer animation and miniaturization and other special effects wizardry, and we are fascinated by the process that led to the product. Good teachers do the same thing with books.

Writing experiences for teachers

✔ Try your hand at poetry. It can rhyme or not—you choose. First, quickly re-read Brod Bagert's poem on page 78, which illustrates the character quality of goodness in the life of people on the poet's street. You take another quality—love, patience, kindness, generosity, you name it. Think of someone who embodies that quality. Then write a poem about that person. If you know someone who's a great example of patience, write your poem so that it illustrates patience without ever using the word itself. Write it so that someone could read the poem and know that it was written to illustrate the character quality of patience, even though that word never appeared in the poem.

✔ Think of a writer you enjoy. Someone whose work you really admire. Then brainstorm why you like that author so much, and what that author does that you could copy in a story, a poem, or just a paragraph. Make notes on what you would like to write about tomorrow, and how your writing will copy the style or subject matter or voice of this writer. Some writers don't like to copy the style of another. But Susan Shaughnessy (1993) tells how you can benefit and why it's not the same as plagiarism:

> How can you tell the difference between helping yourself too liberally to someone else's literary trick and emulating honorably? Something inside you will know the answer.
>
> We learn by copying. Children copy, with their entire bodies, a gesture or stance that enthralls them. They project themselves upon their heroes, and take a little away for their own of what they have admired.
>
> Writers do that, too. If something touches or amuses you in someone else's writing, study it carefully. Return to it several times. Soak it into your intellectual skin.
>
> What you'll get back will not be a carbon copy, but your own interpretation of an old elegance of storytelling. (p. 136).

Review yesterday's brainstorming. Now write.

✔ Reread Sebastian Junger's description of the waterfront in Gloucester, Massachusetts, on page 44. Note his attention to sensory detail. Now pick a scene you know well—perhaps the playground of your school, or your street, or dinnertime at a fast-food restaurant. Try to describe that place using the same techniques Junger used to describe Gloucester.

Classroom experiences for young writers

RuthAnn Shauf, a writing resource teacher, knows that writers learn technique and get ideas by reading the work of authors they love. She does it with her own writing. After she read Margaret Wise Brown's (1949) *The Important Book,* she sat down and wrote her own "important book" about her husband, sons, pets, and, of course, herself. The next day she shared her book with her fourth-graders. Her innovation on this classic book showed students that even their teacher gets ideas from books that she reads. So her 9- and 10-year old kids followed her example and created their own personal—and very important—books, all made possible because they read *The Important Book* like writers.

When RuthAnn assessed her student writers, she discovered that they needed to learn how to develop events in a story in such a way that readers would have a clear picture of what happened. So she looked for a model that would show them how to do this.

RuthAnn launches her writing workshops with books that demonstrate the writing craft she wants her students to learn, so she chose Paul Goble's (1988) *Iktomi and the Boulder* to read aloud, to show how the events in the story made it interesting and created strong visual images. Her students listened with rapt attention as they heard the story of how Iktomi tricked various animals into helping him try to take back the blanket from the boulder. Following the read-aloud, RuthAnn helped her students to recall story events and identify them as part of the beginning, middle, or end of the story.

In the next part of her workshop, she worked with her students to collaborate in writing a new event to add to the story. She re-read one event to the students, asking them to listen with "writer's ears" and then pointed out the techniques Goble had used to help them visualize the action in the story. For their shared writing, they chose to write about having wild horses come along and help Iktomi try to take back the blanket. After they wrote this story event, they read it aloud and agreed, with grins and pride, that it was every bit as good as Goble's.

Knowing that her students must be able to apply this technique in their own writing for the state writing assessment, she provided time for them to practice. She also knew that several of her students were not ready to do this on their own, so she carefully placed students in small groups to collaborate on writing another event for the story. A steady buzz of talk permeated the room as students discussed what they wanted to happen in their event. Soon, the talk slowed as the ideas discussed made their way to pencil and paper. Circulating around the room, RuthAnn stopped to conference briefly with groups.

As writing groups finished up, they began to read their writing aloud. Young writers commented with approval and made suggestions for word changes as groups prepared to share their new parts of the story.

RuthAnn paired groups for sharing and feedback and the room was abuzz. They listened attentively to each other and asked questions, commenting reader to writer and writer to writer. They understood and used the process.

Later that afternoon, RuthAnn shared some of the new pieces with her teacher friends. They laughed together and marveled at the accomplishments of the students. As they discussed the progress and additional practice needed, Sally Stephens, another writing resource teacher, shared two of her new books as possibilities for future craft lessons.

Their eyes lit up as they read and enjoyed Janet Stevens' (1993) *Coyote Steals the Blanket* and Kim Doner's (1999) *Buffalo Dreams. Coyote Steals the Blanket* is based on a Ute folktale and is similar to *Iktomi and the Boulder,* which made it a good choice for the next workshop.

As they read *Buffalo Dreams,* they found even more examples of language that painted a vivid picture and brought the reader into the story:

> Suddenly, Sarah felt an odd strength fill her. Her hand rose. Although frightened, her voice was steady.
> "Mama buffalo...!" The huge animal paused.
> The children took one step back.
> "Please, don't hurt Joey. He's only a baby." Was she listening?
> "He's only a calf."
> Another step back.
> "Please ... let us go."
> The mother buffalo stared as the children inched backward until they bumped the fence.

Kim Doner used strong verbs and varieties of sentence structures to keep her readers in suspense with this event in *Buffalo Dreams.* The teachers decided to use this in a future lesson to stretch the young writers. RuthAnn and her colleagues enjoy sharing the results of writing workshops and craft lessons with each other, because they can discover what works with their young authors and find new books to help their students read like writers.

Patty Linder, a fourth-grade teacher, finds some different challenges with her young writers. She works with many students who travel with their families as they migrate with the growing seasons to pick crops. They are with her while their families pick the winter oranges and strawberries; then they travel up the eastern seaboard to pick cherries or back to Texas and Mexico. Others of her students live year-round on the farms surrounding her school. She must select books carefully to show all of her students how to read like writers.

Narrative writing is part of the state writing assessment program, so Patty teaches personal narrative writing with Cynthia Rylant's *When I Was Young in the Mountains* (1982). She reads the story with her students to enjoy first. Discussions that follow the reading of the book allow all students to share memories of special places and events in their lives. They reread the book to see how Cynthia Rylant wrote about her special places and times. Knowing the importance of her students making the connection between their memories and the writing techniques, she chooses to allow students enough time to craft pieces that will be taken all the way through the writing process to publication in their own books.

It isn't long before a visitor to her room can pick up books that re-create what it was like to be young in Mexico or on a farm in Michigan or down the highway on a local strawberry farm. When all the books are complete and ready to share with an audience outside the classroom, Patty holds an author's tea for her young writers and their guests. The books and authors are grouped by geography for sharing at the tea. Guests experience a vicarious travelogue as writer after writer shares a favorite part of his or her own book.

What started as reading Cynthia Rylant's wonderful book like a writer has resulted in innovations that show these young writers can write personal narratives. What's more, students know they are writers and are eager to begin their next pieces.

The teachers and young writers in these classrooms are eager to learn more about the craft of writing from published authors in trade books. They are confident because they know they have limitless possibilities and examples to learn from. They know where to find them and how to use them. They have learned to read like writers.

References

Bagert, B. (1997). Unpublished manuscript.

Bernays, A. and Painter, P. (1991). *What if? Writing exercises for fiction writers.* New York: HarperCollins.

Brown, M. (1949). *The important book.* New York: Harper.

Carroll, D. (1995). *A manual of writer's tricks.* New York: Marlowe and Co.

Crichton, M. (1991). *Jurassic park.* New York: Ballentine Publishing Group.

Doner, K. (1999). *Buffalo dreams.* Portland, Ore.: WestWinds Press.

Goble, P. (1988). *Iktomi and the boulder.* New York: Orchard.

Lowry, L. (1993). *The giver.* Boston: Houghton Mifflin.

Rylant, C. (1982). *When I was young in the mountains.* New York: Dutton.

Shaughnessy, S. (1993). *Walking on alligators: A book of meditations for writers.* San Francisco: HarperSanFrancisco.

Stephens, J. (1993). *Coyote steals the blanket.* New York: Holiday House.

Developing Voice:
Every
Writer's Uniqueness

Let's say you know Alfred Hitchcock movies well—all except one, which you haven't seen. And then you see that movie without being told it's a Hitchcock movie. You'll still know. You will recognize the great director's style, even without seeing his name on the credits.

Or perhaps you're a Michael Jordan fan. You would recognize Jordan's unique style of play on the court, even if he were wearing another team's jersey and a mask.

Or maybe you tune into your favorite classical-music radio station and hear a piece of music you don't recognize, but you just know it has to be Mozart.

Or you see a painting in a museum and you don't have to look to see who painted it. It's Picasso. You just know.

How do you recognize Hitchcock and Jordan and Mozart and Picasso? They each have a uniqueness, a style all their own. In writing, that's called voice. It's the writer's fingerprints on a piece—his or her uniqueness. Don Murray (1990) says it's what happens "when we read a written text, *and hear the writer.*" (p. 127).

Encouraging the Development of Voice

When teachers define voice they often sound like the Supreme Court justice who said he couldn't define pornography, but he knew it when he saw it. And actually, applied to writing, that's a pretty good way to determine if a piece has voice. You just know.

But if you want to get a little more specific, Vicki Spandel and Richard Stiggins (1997) define voice as "liveliness, passion, energy, awareness of audience, involvement in the topic, and a capacity to elicit a strong response from the reader." (p. 45). They say that a piece of writing with strong voice shows the following characteristics: it sounds like a person wrote it, not a committee; it sounds like *this* particular person; it brings the topic to life; it makes the reader feel connected with the writer—maybe even want to know the writer; it makes the reader respond to the piece and care what happens; the writer seems involved, not bored with the piece; and the writing brims with energy. (p. 50).

So how do you develop voice, and how do you help student writers develop it? Let's begin with the conditions that allow voice to manifest itself. What type of writers, young or old, write with voice?

- *Voice is fostered by fluency:* A fluent writer is one who is accustomed to writing, who writes a lot. When writing becomes a familiar, daily event in someone's life, it is no longer intimidating. Remember the first few times you drove alone in a car as a new teen-age driver? You were nervous and conscious of each little decision you made behind the wheel. Now driving is second nature to you. You listen to the radio, think about what's going on in your life, perhaps talk on a cell phone or apply makeup or even read while you drive. You are comfortable with the act of driving because you've done so much of it. You're a *fluent* driver. Writers achieve fluency by writing a lot in a positive and supportive writing atmosphere. Writers who are not comfortable with the process constantly second-guess themselves and stop in the middle of paragraphs to re-cast the sentence or rewrite the paragraph or maybe just check the spelling of a word. In so doing, they lose their personal connection with the piece and their syntactic thread. Fluent writers—who are more likely to let words flow onto the page because they are comfortable with the writing process—are also typically more likely to express their unique voice in writing.

- *Voice is best expressed in authentic writing:* Authentic means *real*. It's meaningful work done for genuine purposes. It's something we care about. Donald Graves (1984) explains it this way: "Writers do need to learn to choose a topic, limit it, learn what they know and present it to other audiences. The personal base is the base of voice." (p. 191) You are more likely to manifest the real you—voice—when you are writing about something you know about and care about.

- *Writers who enjoy and recognize the voice of other writers are more likely to develop voice themselves:* Most writers can detect voice in their reading long before they manifest it in their writing. And if they are fortunate enough to have a writing teacher who points out the author's voice in the books they are reading and shows them how different authors speak with unique voices, they are more likely to show their own uniqueness on paper.

- *Writers can best develop voice when they seek to be themselves in print:* In other words, they write to express, not to impress. While they might study the style of another, they tell stories and pass along information in their own unique style. Laura Backes (2000) writing in the online writer's newsletter *Inkspot,* explained how writing naturally—like we speak—can let our voice show clearly.

> The best voices appear when authors write as they speak. Has a story ever sounded profound and lyrical in your head, but lost something when you put it on paper? That's because in your head you're telling the story to yourself in your speaking voice, and when you write it down suddenly you're trying to be a writer. You go searching through the thesaurus for the perfect word, something you'd never use in normal conversation. You use three words of description, just because you can, rather than one word that really says everything you need to say. And suddenly in that process of writing down what's in your head, you've lost your voice. You've adapted the voice of someone else, or the voice you think your writing should have. So next time you write, try writing exactly what's in your head. If you type, try typing your writing exercise with your eyes closed, so you can't see the computer screen. Closing your eyes also helps you focus inward where the story is being conceived. Then you'll be guided by how the words sound and feel, and that's the closest thing to your true voice.

So how do you develop voice in yourself or your students? First you must be fluent—accustomed to and comfortable with writing. Then, you must write about what you know and care about. You should take time to appreciate voice as you read other writers. And finally, you should just be yourself in print.

And then what? Wait. Voice is what happens to a writer who writes a lot under the circumstances discussed in this book. You don't *decide* to write with voice. It just happens.

Voice is characteristic of mature authors who write in an affirming atmosphere that encourages them to take risks. You can create an atmosphere in which voice can develop, but you can't rush this aspect of the writing process. You'll never develop voice, for instance, in writers who haven't achieved fluency or who aren't comfortable with the writing process.

Remember also that no writer has one voice exclusively in everything he or she writes. You would have one voice in writing a short story, another in writing a letter of appeal to the IRS, another in writing your master's thesis, and still another in writing a love letter. In the same way that you can go into your closet and choose whether to wear a suit or a pair of jeans, depending on the occasion, writers can choose among the voices that make up their writing style. We do, however, frequently fall into a prevalent voice which affects most things we write. Someone who writes in a very conversational, familiar voice would certainly write a short story or a poem in that voice. But that voice typically also effects even business letters or scholarly articles. And when that person writes a business letter, you can definitely tell it's a business letter; but even that will tend to be more conversational than someone's letter whose voice was more formal to begin with.

So don't be concerned if you can't detect a unique voice in your own writing yet. Just write. Concentrate on the other aspects of good writing you've been reading about in this book. And one day you'll discover—probably because someone tells you after reading something you wrote—that your personality and uniqueness are showing through in your writing.

Writing experiences for teachers

We've already said that voice is something that happens to writers who are developing fluency and thus becoming more comfortable with their writer's craft. So what kind of writing suggestions can we give to develop a quality we've just said isn't really teachable?

One of our suggestions, remember, was to write about what you know. To write authentic pieces about subject matter that's second-nature to you as a writer.

Nothing fills the bill better than writing about our own childhood. The possibilities here are endless. So write about some of the significant events and people of your childhood.

Like what? If your pump needs priming, here are some ideas. Write about: your favorite childhood playmate; the pet you remember best; something you were good at; something you were not good at; your most memorable teacher; the first paying job you ever had; your most embarrassing moment; your most triumphant moment; your experience with athletics; your experience with music; your first kiss; your first sexual experience; your senior prom; how you learned to drive, etc. Just write. Pretend you are telling a close friend, whom you want to know about these people and events. Someone you don't have to try to impress. Really try to be yourself on paper. You may well soon note that you are developing a unique storytelling voice.

And if you aren't? Don't worry. It's probably because you're just not comfortable enough yet as a writer. Keep on writing; it will come.

Classroom experiences for young writers
by Vicki Spandel

Vicki Spandel is a former language arts teacher, technical writer, award-winning video producer, and journalist. Vicki was co-director of the teacher team that developed the six-trait approach to writing, and for more than 17 years, she has taught six-trait writing in seminars throughout the nation. Vicki is author of The Daybooks of Critical Reading and Writing, 3-5; Books, Lessons and Ideas for Teaching the Six Traits; *and* Creating Writers.

> A teacher I know recently defined voice as the "tone that lets me know an author in an intimate way—and helps me decide whether or not to trust that person with the next 300 pages of my life."

That definition strikes me as particularly profound because it shows voice not only as an extension of the writer's own perspective and spirit, but also as the bridge between the writer and reader—that special bond that invites us to trust that information to be shared will be sure, rich, significant, and true.

Often, teachers say voice is the most difficult characteristic of good writing to teach. I find it not only the easiest, but also the most rewarding: voice makes writing more readable, and it gives many young authors (who aren't proficient in organizing information or crafting complex sentences) a place to shine. They feel like writers. For us as teachers, this moment is everything.

Voice can be taught in many ways, but none of them is more important than modeling. Let your own voice out, through your expressive reading, energetic comments, and most of all, by writing with students and showing them the way. Don't be afraid to begin with junk. All writers produce lots of junk along with the good stuff, and letting students see your voice emerge as you revise is invaluable.

So begin roughly: *One day I had a scary experience.* This kind of vague, uninspired writing makes sense in a general way, but it lacks the detail and passion that together produce voice: *As the six-ton gravel truck barreled down upon us, I thought I had but seconds to live—and my only chance was to leap for the cactus.*

Voicy writing produces movies in the reader's mind, often bringing with it sights, sounds, smells, echoes of memories, connections to the reader's own feelings. But it only helps to talk about these things if you share them. *The car smelled awful* is a clear statement, but fairly dull; it lacks voice because it evokes no feelings or associations. Compare: *I got in, and my first thought after fighting for breath was that someone, very long ago, must have purchased a package of hamburger and forgotten it in the trunk.*

Read aloud—often, and from many sources. Examples from professionals like Roald Dahl (*The Twits* [1981], *Boy* [1991]) or Gary Paulsen (*The Winter Room,* [1989] *Harris and Me* [1993]) are invaluable. Other personal favorites (for me) include Rick Bragg's (1997) *All Over But the Shoutin',* Laurie Halse Anderson's (1990) *Speak,* and Kevin Henkes' (1990) *Julius, the Baby of the World.* Think of the books you love and those you love to read aloud, and you'll come up with a dozen examples.

Don't forget pieces that are weak in voice. Nothing teaches so quickly as contrast. Legal contracts, greeting cards, some textbook passages, and much educational and business writing is seriously lacking in voice. Not that legal contracts and textbooks should be chatty. But all writing should speak clearly and without ambiguity to the audience for whom it is intended. And genre is not a predictor of voice—check out informational writing that rings with voice by such authors as Lewis Thomas, Carl Sagan, David Quammen, and Sneed B. Collard.

Another key to voice is passion for the topic. Bored writers produce bored readers. But boredom is a luxury writers can't afford, not if they wish to be successful. Let your students know this—and encourage questions. All topics, from pyramids to warts, are fascinating if we learn to ask and to answer (in our writing) the right questions. Are warts contagious? How would one look under a jeweler's glass? Do warts serve any useful purpose? Can animals get warts, too? Writers typically choose their own topics. But we must also show children how to personalize a topic someone else assigns—to make it their own. That way, when someone hands them a "boring" topic (there's no such thing, in reality), they won't shrug and dash off ho-hum prose, but think to themselves, "How do I wake up uninterested readers with the inside scoop on the pyramids?"

We must teach students to think like writers. In other words, to beware of the audience. Voice must be appropriate to the piece and appropriate to the audience. Voice must suit the audience. Ask students to write on one topic—perhaps "How to Write a Good E-mail"—for several audiences: young children, business people, or those new to the world of electronic mail. Or try a complaint letter about cafeteria food—to the school board or to a friend in another city. Talk about the difference in the voices. And as you share your writing, ask students to define *your* voice (sharp, sarcastic, humorous, polite, timid, etc.) and your audience. Ask them to do the same with peers in response groups. Make the voice/audience connection a part of every piece of writing you produce or share.

Finally, nurture any moment of voice you see in students' writing, no matter how tiny or short-lived. Don't expect resounding voice through a whole piece. It's asking too much. Student writers, like most of us, start out with occasional moments of strength and gradually build to a sustained, powerful voice.

At first, voice in student writing comes and goes. So what? Look for the high points. Respond. Be enthusiastic. That's how you get more. As a first-year teacher, I rejoiced when my shiest student wrote, "They try to get me down with their comments and their criticisms. They try to be mean to me. But I just keep on truckin'." I was dancing through the halls in my excitement. This timid student who never spoke in class, who rarely wrote at all, was sharing his inner thoughts. For him, it was a major victory. I marked the line with a "Good for you! Go get 'em!" and showed it to a veteran teacher who was my mentor at the time. She smiled at me indulgently. "You'll get over being so easily impressed," she told me. Thankfully, she was wrong. I continue to be impressed by my students' work and by their courage to share—and I let them know it.

Why not? If moments of voice lurked within your writing, would you not want to know you had touched someone? Let your students know (Your voice really touched me—right here—and here ...) and ask for their feedback on your own writing in return. Within a community of writers, voice blossoms. Guess what? As your students' voice grows, so will yours.[1]

Note

1. If you would like to read a scholarly examination of voice that deals with the issues introduced in this chapter in much more depth, get Kathleen Blake Yancey's (1994) book *Voices on Voice.*

References

Anderson, L. (1999). *Speak.* New York: Farrar, Straus and Giroux.

Backes, L. (2000). "Finding your voice as a children's writer," *Inkspot.* http://www.inkspot.com/feature/voice.html.

Bragg, R. (1997). *All over but the shoutin'.* New York: Pantheon.

Dahl, R. (1981). *The twits.* New York: Puffin Books.

Dahl, R. (1991). *Boy.* New York: Penguin USA.

Henkes, K. (1990). *Julius, the baby of the world.* New York: Greenwillow.

Graves, D. (1984). *A researcher learns to write.* Portsmouth, NH: Heinemann.

Murray, D. (1990). *Shoptalk: Learning to write with writers.* Portsmouth, NH: Boynton/Cook.

Paulsen, G. (1989). *The winter room.* New York: Orchard Books.

Paulsen, G. (1993). *Harris and me.* New York: Bantam Doubleday Dell.

Spandel, V, and Stiggins, R. (1997). *Creating writers: Linking writing assessment and instruction.* New York: Longman.

Yancey, Kathleen Blake (ed). (1994). *Voices on voice: Perspectives, definitions, inquiry.* Urbana, Ill: National Council of Teachers of English.

Writing Expository Text:
It's Easier
Than You Think

Some writers—and writing teachers—find narrative and story much easier than expository writing. They have become accustomed to the skills and techniques of narrative, and they are not sure exactly how to approach writing whose purpose it is to explain or persuade or contrast.

So here's the good news: the techniques of expository are basically the same as the techniques of story. For instance, let's say you have a chef who is known for baking excellent cakes but has never baked a pie. Does he have to completely re-educate himself to achieve excellence in baking pies? Not at all. Pies and cakes look different and taste different and use different ingredients. But the same principles of baking apply. Many of the same ingredients are used. The similarities are so significant that if you can bake a great German Chocolate cake, there's no reason you can't also bake a mouth-watering apple pie.

Everything we've already looked at in this book—from leads to dialogue to strong verbs—applies equally to expository pieces as to narratives and stories. Learning to write effective factual pieces involves only the application of those techniques to a different genre.

Using the Techniques of Story in Expository Text

Some writers are daunted by the sheer range of expository text, which includes description, directions, compare-contrast, persuasive, essay, advertisement, and lots more. It isn't necessary to study each classification of expository separately since all use basically the same techniques. But here's what is necessary:

Writers of any age who have achieved fluency (that is, they are accustomed to writing on a regular basis and see themselves as writers) can more easily switch genres: You might enjoy writing stories much more than writing expository text, but you should be able to achieve a similar level of facility, if not enjoyment, on both. Don't just assume that your students will enjoy story more than expository, either. Remember, many of the books they enjoy most are expository texts – books about the ocean or dinosaurs or ancient Egypt or pirates or African animals or UFOs or anacondas.

We need to read expository like writers, to look for characteristics of good expository writing in the books we enjoy: Marcia Freeman, a Florida writing teacher, calls this "developing an ear for expository." Freeman (1997) writes:

> When we read to children, nine times out of ten we read fiction. While this helps them develop an ear for story, it inadvertently implies that expository writing is less interesting, less exciting, and less important than fiction. By neglecting to read expository literature, we miss the opportunity to help our students get a feeling for and an appreciation of the genre.
>
> Just as students develop an ear and a preference for different styles of music, so can they develop and ear and preference for different genres of writing. You can help your students become better expository writers by reading well-written expository samples to them. (p. 2).

As you begin to think about expository writing, don't get bogged down by the number of different forms that writing may take. Most expository writing falls into one of two categories: Writing that presents facts or information, and writing deals with opinion. Every writing technique in this book is as applicable to expository as it is to story and narrative.

So what's the big difference between expository and story/narrative? Primarily, it's organization. Stories and narratives are organized chronologically. Sometimes we violate a strict chronology with flashbacks or beginning close to the conflict and using dialogue and other techniques to gradually fill in the reader on what has gone on before we started telling the story. But even then, most narratives and stories follow a basically chronological format.

Expository writing, on the other hand, typically organizes by placing related information together. We might write a letter to the editor arguing for approval of a new tax for school construction, offering three reasons we think voters should approve the measure. No matter who's writing the letter, the organization will probably be the same: a thesis statement, that voters should approve the tax; the three reasons we think it should be approved; and some sort of summary statement, perhaps expanding our strongest argument or offering an illustration of the benefits of the tax passage or the dire consequences if it isn't.

How would the other techniques you've been working on apply to this expository text? For instance, you'd want to write a lead that grabbed the reader's attention. Why start with, "I urge voters to approve the proposed tax increase for school construction in this Saturday's election" when you can write something like this:

> Jimmy Walker has attended Franklin Elementary School for three years, but he has never had a class inside the building. Jimmy is one of hundreds of students who go to classes in drafty

> portable buildings and have to put on heavy coats during the winter just to visit the library or go to the lunchroom. And Jimmy is one of the reasons we need to approve the proposed tax increase for new school construction this Saturday.

And the *show, don't tell* maxim applies as much for expository as it does for story. You wouldn't want to write about the alarming number of older buildings (what's *alarming?* and how old is *older?*) still in use in your city's schools when you could point out that half of your elementary schools were built in the 1950's.

You can get a daily dose of expository text by reading newspapers and magazines. In the news sections, you find articles that distill, abstract, and summarize information. On the editorial and op-ed pages, there are persuasive pieces, humor columns, and essays. In feature sections, look for process descriptions (how-to-do-it pieces) and informational articles (feature stories) on non-news events. And if you think of expository text as dry, read pop-culture biographical essays in *People* or *Biography*. Or science features in *Popular Science* or *Scientific American*. Or how-to-do-it pieces in *Money* or *Better Homes and Gardens*.[1]

Writing experiences for teachers

✔ Since one of the examples you just read dealt with how to use principles of good writing in a letter to the editor, let's start with that. If we've caught you a little unprepared to write one, go ahead and read today's instructions and put them on your mental back-burner to simmer for a few days. Then go ahead to some of the other writing experiences in this section. And as you write other things, be on the lookout for topics for your letter.

As you think about a letter, think in terms of medium and message. What medium would you like to send it to? A local or regional newspaper? A newsmagazine? A professional newspaper or magazine? A specialized (hobby, sport, fashion) magazine? And don't forget on-line letters to the editor that might not be printed in the print product but might be featured on a Web site. Even a posting on an Internet listserv would qualify here. Is it really necessary to really send it off for potential publication? It is if you want to get the maximum benefit from what you write.

After you've identified a medium, the message should be easy. Just look over a recent issue of the publication and comment on a news event, the publication's coverage of that event, an editorial or column in the publication, or another letter to the editor written by someone else. The possibilities are endless.

✔ Today try a process description (a how-to-do-it). Make it practical. You might write a set of instructions on how to boot up classroom computers, access the word-processing software, open a new text file, save, and exit the system. Or maybe write a letter to parents on how they can maximize the time they spend reading to their children or how to help with math homework without taking over from the child and doing it themselves. Or just

how the home can cooperate with the school to maximize their child's learning experience.

✔ Write two short paragraphs. First, pick an issue about which you are fairly
familiar. Maybe the pro-life vs. pro-choice debate or intensive systematic
phonics vs. balanced literacy as a philosophy on reading pedagogy. It could
even be California vs. Florida as an ideal vacation destination. Then write a
paragraph in which you advocate one side as well as you can. Then write
another taking exactly the opposite view. Try to make both equally effective.

✔ Write a letter to an imaginary first-year teacher. Tell this new teacher what
he or she didn't learn in school of education classes and will have to learn in
the real world of the classroom. You'll probably never do anything with this
letter, but it should be the kind of letter you wish you had received before
you started teaching—things you had to learn the hard way, on your own.
Use the techniques we've been looking at. Instead of just telling about hard-
to-get-along-with parents, for example, throw in some dialogue from your
first conversation with an intransigent parent.[1]

Classroom applications

by Marcia Freeman

*Marcia Freeman, formerly a high school science and elementary teacher, is a
writing educational consultant. She is the author of several books on teaching
writing, including* Listen to this; Developing an ear for expository *(1997). She is
also the author of children's fiction, photo-illustrated science and geography big
books, and non-fiction guided reading books.*

An emergent writer's first and natural writing mode is personal and informational. It is expository writing.

This is my house.
I love my mom. I love my grandpa. I love my
teacher. I love my teddy bear.
I have a dog and he acts like a puppy.
This is my rabbit. She eats carrots. And she
likes me.

Expository writing is about information or ideas. It is commu-
nicating feelings, explaining, giving directions, expressing opinions, and persuading. It is the genre of literature response, reading comprehension questions, and academic test questions. It is
the genre of the workaday world. Almost everything almost
everyone writes is expository.

- *Help children find personal topics:* Model how to list personal expertise topics for your students. List things you know about, places you have been, things you can do. Include a few science/social studies topics your students have studied in class, but mainly list out-of-school knowledge and activities: fishing, making toast, biking, jumping rope, dogs, grandmother, whales, singing, drawing pigs, dancing, coloring books, fire engines, museums, parks, TV programs, shopping, and so forth.

  Give your students a long strip of cardstock (a heavy weight of paper)—a list should look and feel like a list—and help them write a list of their areas of personal expertise. Emergent writers can construct one with pictures—pasted or drawn. Provide time for students to listen to each other's lists. Interview those who are having difficulty making one. Ask them about their games, their chores, their after-school activities. Help them find the things about which they have personal knowledge and experience.

- *Elaboration comes from knowing your subject:* We want young writers to elaborate on their ideas. First and second graders should be able to write several paragraphs of related information on a topic; third graders, more. Elaboration in writing is directly proportional to the writer's depth of knowledge about a topic. Writing about what they know best will help young writers elaborate.

- *Use personal writing as the vehicle for skill-building:* When children write about themselves, they are engaged and emotionally connected to their subject. There are no knowledge barriers. They can place almost their entire attention on the writing itself. They can learn to apply writing skills associated with informational writing such as *question or exclamation hooks, descriptive details, comparisons, specificity, and endings that tell how they feel about the topic.*

- *Support young writers' natural mode with your read-aloud program:* Develop your students' ear for the expository genre. Read books on a theme; first an informational book on the topic, then a story. For instance, you might read an article or a science big book about eggs hatching, and follow that with P.D. Eastman's *Are You My Mother,* an appealing classic story of a hatchling who came out of his shell while his mother was off the nest, and who asks everyone and everything, "Are you my mother?"

- *Read aloud children's picture books that are not stories—* not organized chronologically. Some examples are:

  - *Come out, Muskrats,* by Jim Aronsky (1993). New York: Dutton.
  - *Cows,* by Peter Brady (1996). Minnesota: Capstone Press.
  - *Dogs,* by Gail Gibbons (1996). New York: Holiday House.
  - *I Am an Artist,* by Pat Lowery Collins (1992). Connecticut: Millbrook Press.
  - *Me and My Map,* by Joan Sweeny (1996). New York: Crown Publishers.
  - *Push and Pull,* by Marcia Freeman (1997). New York: Newbridge.
  - *The Tortilla Factory,* by Gary Paulsen (1995). New York: Harcourt Brace.
  - *Twilight Comes Twice,* by Ralph Fletcher (1997). New York: Clarion.
  - *Urban Roosts,* by Barbara Bash (1995). Boston: Little, Brown.
  - *Wetlands,* by Marcia Freeman (1997). New York: Newbridge.

- *Read non-fiction big books:* articles from *Junior National Geographic, Ranger Rick,* and *Ladybug* magazine, directions to games, advertisements, invitations, letters to be sent home, book reviews, and the "about the author" information from fiction books you read to your class.

- *And check out the new primary reading series appearing on the market:* They are non-fiction and photo-illustrated, focus on science and social studies concepts, consisting of emergent, developing, and fluent levels.

  When you read informational books, not only do children develop an ear for the expository genre, but they also learn facts about nature, science, history, social studies, cooking, art, music, books, sports, etc. Your reading aloud does double-duty.

- *Use expository writing vocabulary:* Refer to emergent writers' informational writing as *your writing, your piece, your picture/writing,* or *your manuscript.* Do not call their writing *a story,* as in *Bring your story to author's chair;*

Let me hear your story; What is your story about?, etc. Unless, of course, you know it is a story.

When children share their piece in author's chair, encourage them to say: *This is what I know about dogs; This is what I saw at the zoo; This is what I know about manatees; This is an information piece;* or *This is expository writing.*

Note

1. To investigate this genre further as a writer, read William Zinsser's (1988) *Writing to Learn.* To read about expository texts from the perspective of both a writer and a writing teacher, try Donald Graves' (1989) *Investigate Nonfiction.* You can find excellent ideas for teaching expository techniques in the classroom in Marcia Freeman's (1997) *Listen to This: Developing an Ear for Expository.*

References

Aronsky, Jim (1993). *Come out, muskrats.* New York: Dutton.

Bash, Barbara (1995). *Urban roosts.* Boston: Little, Brown.

Brady, Peter (1996). *Cows.* Minnesota: Capstone Press.

Collins, Pat Lowery (1992). *I am an artist.* Connecticut: Millbrook Press.

Fletcher, Ralph (1997). *Twilight comes twice.* New York: Clarion.

Freeman, M. (1997). *Listen to this: Developing an ear for expository.* Gainesville, Fla.: Maupin House.

Freeman, Marcia (1997). *Push and pull.* New York: Newbridge.

Freeman, Marcia (1997). *Wetlands.* New York: Newbridge.

Gibbons, Gail (1996). *Dogs.* New York: Holiday House.

Graves, D. (1989). *Investigate nonfiction.* Portsmouth, NH: Heinemann.

Paulsen, Gary (1995). *The tortilla factory.* New York: Harcourt Brace.

Sweeny, Joan (1996). *Me and my map.* New York: Crown Publishers.

Zinsser, W. (1988). *Writing to learn.* New York: Harper & Row.

A Final Word: Can Writing Be Taught?

The debate is as old as writing instruction: Can writing be taught, or must it just be learned by the would-be writer's trial-and-effort experience?

The authors of this book agree with both sides in this debate. Writing can indeed be taught, but students do not really become writers—or improve as writers—until they take what they have been taught and apply it daily to a number of writing situations.

Look at the writing teacher as a gardener planting a seed. Does she cause the seed to germinate and to grow into a beautiful flower? No, but she plays an important role. She plants the seed in the right type of soil and the right sunlight conditions. She fertilizes it and waters it. She prunes the plant and does everything necessary to keep it healthy. The gardener didn't make the plant grow, but she provided the conditions—the environment—in which it could grow.

And that's what good writing teachers do. They provide a writer-friendly classroom atmosphere that's conducive to the growth of writing skills. If you visit the classrooms of good writing teachers, here's what you will find them doing:

- *They expose students to good writing:* Their rooms are full of books and print, and they frequently read aloud from their favorites.

- *They share their excitement about good writing:* It may be a paragraph written by a student or something they find and share in a novel they are reading. Students know these teachers love books and beautiful language—and they know they get excited over effective writing.

- *They offer students time to write in workshop conditions:* Writing is an everyday activity in their classes, and they write across the curriculum.

- *They model writing:* They write for their students and with their students. Students know that these teachers are writers, too.

- ***They use assessment to inform their instruction:*** They assess what their writers are doing, and they help young writers to self-assess their work. That assessment then leads to craft lessons and other classroom activities designed to meet the needs of their writers.

- ***They teach conventions—grammar, spelling, punctuation, usage—but they teach them in the content of writing:*** Their students see the conventions as tools used by writers, not isolated skills.

- ***They give their students an audience through publication:*** Their students see themselves as writers because they have opportunities to write for real readers in the classroom and beyond.

This book was designed to help you use the literature in your class—the literature your students already love—to teach writing. As you build lessons from that literature and do it in the type of classroom atmosphere described above, your students will grow as writers.

And you will see your students come to love writing—because *you* do.

About the Authors

Tommy Thomason is a former professional journalist who is now chairman of the Department of Journalism at Texas Christian University in Fort Worth. He also brings the perspective of a professional writer into elementary school classrooms, where he conducts writing workshops with children every week. Dr. Thomason is the author of *More Than a Writing Teacher: How to Become a Teacher Who Writes* and *Writer to Writer: How to Conference Young Authors.* He and Carol York co-authored *Write on Target: Preparing Young Writers to Succeed on State Writing Achievement Tests.*

Carol York is a former elementary classroom teacher who taught students in grades one through six and Title I Reading. Her experience also includes service as supervisor of Title I Evaluation and Title I Reading. Ms. York is currently supervisor of elementary language arts for the School District of Hillsborough County in Tampa, Florida. She is co-author of *Write on Target: Preparing Young Writers to Succeed on State Writing Achievement Tests.*

Author and Subject Index